THE COMPLETE NFL COOKBOOK

Compiled by Hyla O'Connor
Drawings by Roseanne Litzinger

A National Football League Publication

A PLUME BOOK
NEW AMERICAN LIBRARY
TIMES MIRROR
NEW YORK AND SCARBOROUGH, ONTARIO

**PLUME TRADEMARK REG. U.S. PAT. OFF. AND FOREIGN
COUNTRIES
REGISTERED TRADEMARK—MARCA REGISTRADA
HECHO EN CRAWFORDSVILLE, INDIANA, U.S.A.**

NAL books are available at discounts in bulk quantity for
industrial or sales-promotional use. For details, write to
Premium Marketing Division, New American Library, Inc.,
1633 Broadway, New York, New York 10019.

© 1981 by National Football League Properties, Inc.
All rights reserved. For information, address The New American
Library, Inc.

SIGNET, SIGNET CLASSICS, MENTOR, PLUME, MERIDIAN, '
and NAL BOOKS are published by
The New American Library, Inc.
1633 Broadway, New York, New York 10019

ISBN: 0-452-25298-9
Library of Congress Catalog Number: 81-81901
First Printing, September 1981

1   2   3   4   5   6   7   8   9

PRINTED IN THE UNITED STATES OF AMERICA

CONTENTS

INTRODUCTION
COOKING WITH THE PROS

An NFL cookbook? It isn't as far-fetched as it may seem at first. Ask any of the country's thousands of tailgate party aficionados and they'll tell you that football and food go together like...well, football and food!

From August through the Super Bowl the NFL season provides a variety of opportunities for entertaining—at home, in backyards and parks, and in stadium parking lots. As more and more fans have developed a taste for football-related hosting, a certain style has developed right along with it, a style that allows the cook to enjoy the guests and the game instead of spending the first half in the kitchen cheering on slow-boiling pots.

Each year it seems that cooking for tailgate and Monday night get-togethers gains in popularity. Reflecting this rising national trend in "football cooking" are numerous NFL players, coaches, front office people, and teams—right up to NFL Commissioner Pete Rozelle—from whom most of the recipes in this book were gathered.

Consider Philadelphia Eagles quarterback Ron Jaworski. In 1977, when the Eagles announced the acquisition of Jaworski from the Los Angeles Rams, they threw a little party for the press. The featured item—besides Jaworski, of course—was stuffed cabbage. Thus, a fitting ethnic food heralded a new chapter in the career of the player known as the "Polish Rifle."

Since that signing, Jaworski has led the Eagles into the NFC playoffs three times and to Super Bowl XV, in addition to establishing himself as one of the top quarterbacks in the game today. Although he hasn't attributed his success to stuffed cabbage, he continues to be a connoisseur of Polish food.

Another NFL quarterback calling culinary signals is Joe Theismann of the Washington Redskins. Theismann, who became the Redskins' starting quarterback in the 1979 season, keeps up a frenetic pace in his off-field activities. Among other things, he co-hosts a Washington, D.C., television show, makes numerous personal appearances, and presides over the restaurant that bears his name in Baileys Crossroads, Virginia. Although Theismann stays out of the restaurant's kitchen during busy hours, he occasionally sends in a recipe, so to speak, from the sideline.

There's a lot of culinary talent on the four-time Super Bowl champion Pittsburgh Steelers. Some of the Steelers, such as defensive tackle Steve Furness, recently retired safety Mike Wagner, and wide receiver Lynn Swann show their winning style in the kitchen as well as on the field.

Furness specializes in breakfast and egg dishes. This is partly because he likes them, he says, but also because morning cooking fits in with his busy schedule.

"I have a heavy offseason training program, and eating is one of the basics of it," says Furness. "I get up early in the morning and lift weights and work out, so I do a lot of the breakfast-making in the house, particularly on weekends."

Wagner likes to do his cooking later in the day. He says he used to threaten to really cook for his teammates, but that he kept it simple with them, serving mainly barbecued steaks and hamburgers.

But there was one time, he recalls, when the cooking in his house got as competitive as the Super Bowl.

"Lynn Swann was over," says Wagner, "and he and my daughter Heather were talking about cooking. Somehow the conversation got around to Chicken Kiev, and Heather bragged that her mother Cathy made it really well. Swann said that he cooked it, too. One thing led to another and Lynn and Cathy ended up having a Chicken Kiev cookoff with Heather as the judge."

Who won? "Heather's a diplomat,"

Wagner says with a laugh. "She wouldn't say whose was better. She was too busy eating as much of both as she could."

St. Louis guard Terry Stieve has another reason for cooking that fits in well with both his place of residence and his occupation. Stieve lives in New Orleans in the offseason.

"Down there," he says, "the Cajuns believe cooking is a measure of manliness. Most all of the men do at least the seafood cooking in the house."

Stieve took his macho credo one step further when he not only did some serious seafood cooking, but did it for the entire Cardinals team and coaching staff in the Terry Stieve Locker Room Oyster Bar.

"I knew just about everyone on the team liked oysters," Stieve explains, "so I called a New Orleans restaurateur friend and asked him to airfreight some oysters up to St. Louis. My friend knows all the good ol' Cajun boys who know where the best oyster beds are. So I was sure he'd send up some good oysters."

Stieve picked up the oysters—400 pounds of them—at the airport and took them back to his house. He kept them overnight in a bath tub covered with 12 bags of ice. The next day he took them to the locker room where, after practice and films, he served them, some raw on the half shell and the rest fried to make oyster poor boys, a southern Louisiana sandwich treat.

In St. Louis, it seems, everybody wants to get into the act—and the kitchen. Billy Bidwill, the team's owner, is co-owner of a restaurant, and at least twice a year, two members of the team's scouting department, Stan West and Bo Bolinger, cook up their specialties, chili and cornbread.

St. Louis, however, is not the only football club with its share of gridiron gourmets. A number of NFL teams have feasting functions. But, when it comes to team functions on the grand scale, the New Orleans Saints are the hands down winners with their Superboil. Sponsored by the Saints Touchdown Club, a booster organization, the

Superboil is a raucous annual event. This giant eating and drinking extravaganza, which is held in April, corresponds with the time that crayfish, the star attraction of the menu, are most abundant. The Superboil also corresponds with the Saints' spring mini-camp for veteran players and is one of the team's major social functions.

More than 400 players, coaches, and fans attended a recent Superboil and gorged themselves on 3,000 pounds of crayfish, 600 stuffed crabs, 150 pounds of potato salad, and 20 kegs of beer.

But if the Saints have the champion team function in terms of size, the New England Patriots are the champions of style. In the fall of 1979 at a game with the Miami Dolphins, the Patriots hosted 80 lucky diners at what has to be the ultimate tailgate party. Prepared by the staff and students of Johnson and Wales College, a renowned cooking school in Providence, Rhode Island, the affair may have raised the pregame cookout to a high art form. The meal, served on linen and silver bedecked tables with candelabra under a green-and-white striped canopy, included paté, caviar, beef tenderloin, and lobster, all washed down with a choice of champagne and selected wines. There also were after-dinner cigars for those desiring them. By the way, the Patriots won the football game 28-13.

Another less sumptuous but no less enjoyable, annual NFL event takes place in that mile-high city famous for ruining cake recipes, Denver. Since 1978, the team has sponsored the Denver Broncos Wives' Annual Taste Luncheon, which has become a favorite institution around Mile-High Stadium. At the luncheon, the participating wives of Broncos players, coaches, and front office personnel all bring their favorite dishes, potluck style. Recipes for all the featured foods are given to those in attendance.

Recipes from the Dallas Cowboys are available in book form. Since 1979, they've put out The Dallas Cowboys Wives' Cookbook and Family Album. A short look through it confirms that, in terms of cooking, the Cowboys' tastes are as widely varied as their offensive formations.

The concept for the Cowboys' cookbook originated with Mary Breunig, wife of all-pro middle linebacker Bob Breunig. The idea was to create a revenue-raising project to benefit a charity. The team decided that all proceeds from the cookbook's sale would go to the Happy Hill Farm Children's Home in Glen Rose, Texas, for children with special learning disabilities and handicaps.

The Chicago Bears' wives also publish a team cookbook to raise money for charity. Their cookbook, The Bear Essentials for Cooking, began simply as a means for wives of Bears personnel to exchange recipes for their favorite dishes.

Of course, cooking for a football team is a lot different than cooking for a family, although sometimes Pat Grant, wife of Minnesota Vikings coach Bud Grant, is hard-pressed to see how. She says she always seems to have more than just her four boys and Bud around the dinner table. More often than not, she cooks for 8 to 10 people, and that's not including her yearly coaches and players pregame tailgate party.

Things are the other way around in the household of Ray Malavasi, the head coach of the Los Angeles Rams. There, he does most of the cooking, especially during the offseason. Malavasi says the reason he took charge in the kitchen is that his wife Mary doesn't like to cook.

"It didn't take me long to find that out," he says. "When we were first married, I brought home some fresh corn. She said, 'What am I supposed to do with this?' I told her to boil it. She did —husks, silk, and all. Another time I brought home some artichokes for dinner. When I went to take them out of the pot, I found that she had picked off all the leaves before cooking them. Then, one time, she made a turkey. I smelled something burning and opened up the oven. She had cooked the gizzards in their paper wrapping."

Since then, few turkeys have gone

up in smoke. In fact, Malavasi is noted for his Thanksgiving spreads. He says he also makes good lasagna and pizza, but the pizza often causes problems with his five children because Ray is the only one in the family who likes anchovies on it.

Malavasi says he gets a lot of his ideas and recipes—particularly his Italian ones—from his mother. Unfortunately, his attempts to duplicate her specialties don't always work out.

"When I was at Memphis State," he says, "I decided I wanted to make some polenta and baccala. Polenta is corn meal and baccala is dried, salted codfish—they look something like baseball bats. My mother used to make it and it was one of my favorites. I couldn't find the baccala anywhere in Memphis, but the guy who ran a little local market ordered a case from Chicago for me. I got it home, soaked it in water, and then tried to cook it in garlic and olive oil. It was terrible! The fish was salty and hard. I couldn't figure out what I had done wrong. So I called my mother. She asked me how long I had soaked the fish. I told her two hours. She laughed and said, 'Ray, you have to soak it for three days!'"

One thing about NFL cooks, they're prepared to ply their avocation anytime and anywhere. A case in point is George Pernicano, a part-owner of the San Diego Chargers, and the full owner of Casa di Baffi, a San Diego restaurant that during the football season is as crowded as the broadcast booth at a Monday night game. The name of the restaurant translates from Italian as "House of the Moustache" and was named for Pernicano's prized 15-inch handlebar that has been insured for $50,000 with Lloyds of London since 1947.

On a trip to an NFL meeting in Hawaii a few years ago, Pernicano's skills made him a gourmet legend among team owners.

"We kept having to go to all these cocktail parties," says Pernicano. "I was eating nothing but hors d'oeuvres and finger food, and I finally got tired of it. So I went out and bought some pots, a hot plate, and bags and bags of groceries

—all of which I sneaked into the hotel and up to my room. Then I started cooking. My room number was ninety-two, so somebody called it 'Club Ninety-Two.' In five days I fed a hundred and twenty-five people, about twenty-five a night on my veranda overlooking the pool and Diamond Head. People would holler up from the pool, 'What's on the menu for today?' We really had to take care of the maid."

And NFL cooks never forget the spirit of competition. There have been challenge matches of all kinds in sports, even in the kitchen, such as the Swann-Wagner Chicken Kiev contest. But few have compared to the barbecue challenge that took place at the Seattle Seahawks' training camp between the team's general manager John Thompson and Hal Childs, then a public relations man for the Seattle Mariners baseball club. It all started when Thompson (or Childs, depending on whose version you believe) began boasting about his prowess as a barbecue chef. There was no way to resolve the issue except with a cookoff.

On the appointed date, with a number of hungry Seahawks players looking on expectantly, the battling barbecue chefs had it out over hot coals with tongs and spatulas. When the hickory smoke had cleared, Thompson and his barbecued pork chops were declared victorious.

"The barbecue was fixed," admits Thompson. "I had the team caterer go out and buy two-inch thick pork chops. They sealed the win. We ended up cooking 119 chops for thirty-nine people. Even so, they went so fast that I didn't even get one."

Now, after all this about the raison d'être for an NFL cookbook, would you like to know the best thing about NFL cooking? You don't need a football game to do it! Long after the Super Bowl is over, you still can enjoy Thompson's pork chops, Pernicano's fettucine, or Stieve's oysters. So, give the recipes and entertaining ideas on the pages that follow a tryout. They're your season ticket to good eating—all year long.

GAME DAY BRUNCHES
PREGAME WARMUPS FOR SUNDAY OR ANY DAY

Brunch, a combination of breakfast and lunch, is as American as football. It has become such a popular meal that restaurants all over the country are serving special brunch menus.

By its nature, brunch is a free-form sort of meal. You can serve almost anything you can think of, though, given the early time of day, it's best to stick with lighter, less rich dishes.

Pick and choose from the recipes offered here, use your own favorites, or organize a "theme" brunch party around one easily varied main dish.

Omelets are good football brunch party fare. They are easy to make and fun to taste with a variety of fillings. Or, try poached eggs served up as Eggs Benedict or Eggs Florentine. Unique sandwiches, hot and cold, also lend themselves well to brunching.

A waffle party makes a perfect pregame brunch. Depending on the size of the party, several waffle irons can be set up at the same time. With the batters all ready, each person can make the kind of waffle he or she wants.

Those fans desiring something as lively as the NFL game they're watching can put together a Mexican brunch that runs the taste gamut from smooth and cool Gazpacho soup to spicy chalupas and enchiladas.

A really different brunch idea is a fondue party. You can serve a cheese fondue, with everyone swirling crisp French bread in the cheese, a beef fondue with a choice of sauces, or a chocolate fondue with pieces of fresh fruit or sponge cake as dippers.

It doesn't matter which type of brunch you serve—they all make the combination of sleeping late and football irresistible.

ROOKIE OMELETS

10 eggs, at room temperature
¾ teaspoon salt
¼ teaspoon pepper
¼ cup butter, divided

1. Combine eggs, salt, and pepper in a bowl. Beat lightly with a fork, just until yolks and whites are combined.

2. Heat 1 tablespoon of butter in an omelet pan over high heat just to the point where the butter begins to turn brown. Add ¼ of the egg mixture and immediately stir briskly with a fork. When eggs have thickened and begun to set on the bottom, stop stirring. With left hand, shake the pan gently back and forth to loosen eggs.

3. Put desired filling in center of omelet. With a fork, fold one-third of omelet over center. Then fold other third in. Slide omelet out of pan onto a heated serving plate. Cut in half and serve at once.

4. Repeat process three more times with the same or different fillings.

Makes eight servings.

TOMATO OMELETS

4 slices bacon
3 ripe tomatoes, peeled and seeded
½ teaspoon salt
½ teaspoon basil
Pinch of sugar
½ teaspoon curry powder
Snipped parsley

1. Fry bacon until crisp. Remove bacon to paper towels and drain.

2. Cut up tomatoes and add to bacon fat in skillet. Cook, stirring occasionally, for about 20 minutes. Add salt, basil, sugar, and curry powder. Add bacon and simmer three minutes.

3. Prepare Rookie Omelets. Add a spoonful of tomato filling to center before folding over. Top with additional filling and sprinkle with snipped parsley.

Makes four servings of filling.

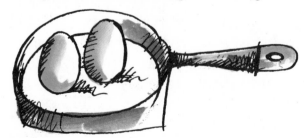

HOTSPURRITO OMELET

1 12-inch flour tortilla
3 eggs
½ cup green pepper, chopped
½ cup onions, chopped
2 tablespoons butter or margarine
½ cup ham, diced
Swiss cheese, shredded
Diced tomatoes or salsa sauce

1. Keep tortilla warm in a very low oven.
2. Beat eggs well. Set aside.
3. Cook pepper and onion in hot butter until tender but not browned. Add ham and cook a few minutes.
4. Heat a little butter in another skillet over high heat. Add beaten eggs and cook, slightly shaking pan several times. Add cooked pepper, onion, and ham and cook until done.
5. Turn out omelet on top of tortilla. Fold over tortilla and top with cheese. Put on a baking sheet and cook under a hot broiler until cheese melts.
6. Serve with tomatoes.
Makes one serving.

Variation: Moonlight Omelet
Add ½ to ¾ cup sauteed mushrooms to the top of omelet. Top with Monterey Jack or Swiss cheese. Broil until bubbly.

STRAWBERRY OMELETS

1 quart fresh strawberries, cleaned and coarsely chopped
2 tablespoons orange juice
Grated rind of ½ orange
¼ cup sugar
Rookie Omelets
4 tablespoons heavy cream

1. Put strawberries in a sauce pan with orange juice, orange rind, and sugar. Bring to a boil. Lower heat and simmer five minutes. Keep warm.
2. When each omelet is cooked, spread 1 tablespoon of the cream over top of omelet. Spoon 3 to 4 tablespoons of berries on top of cream and fold up omelet. Serve with some of the syrup from the berries.
Makes enough filling for eight omelet servings.

17

WILD CARD OMELETS

Green beans, French cut
Broccoli, cut very small
Onion, chopped
Mushrooms, sliced
Zucchini, sliced
Spinach, chopped
Celery, chopped
Green or red pepper, diced
Rookie Omelets
Ham, diced
American or Swiss cheese, sliced

1. Stir-fry any combination of vegetables in a small amount of oil until vegetables are done but still crisp.

2. When each omelet is ready, sprinkle on ham and cheese slices. Top with vegetable mixture, fold, and serve.

EGGS IN A HUDDLE

½ teaspoon anchovy paste
10 tablespoons butter or margarine, divided
4 cups cooked fine egg noodles
6 chicken livers, broiled and chopped
6 eggs
1 cup milk
1 bay leaf
Salt and pepper to taste
1 tablespoon flour
½ cup heavy cream
½ cup Gruyere cheese, grated

1. Blend anchovy paste with 4 tablespoons butter. Melt, then butter six individual casseroles with this mixture.

2. Melt 2 tablespoons butter and toss with cooked noodles. Line each casserole with some of the noodles.

3. Place ⅙ of the chicken livers in each noodle nest. Break an egg into center of nest.

4. Bake in a 350 degree oven for five minutes or until egg just begins to set. Remove from oven.

5. Heat milk with bay leaf and seasonings. Remove bay leaf. Melt 1 tablespoon butter in a saucepan. Add flour and cook and stir for one minute. Stir in strained milk. Cook over medium heat, stirring until mixture is reduced by one third. Stir in cream and cheese until

cheese is melted. Stir in remaining 3 tablespoons butter. Pour 3 tablespoons sauce over each egg nest.

6. Place casseroles on baking sheet. Broil a few inches from heat until nests are lightly browned.

Makes six servings.

EGGS FLORENTINE

1 package (10½ ounces) frozen
   chopped spinach
1 tablespoon butter
2 tablespoons minced onion
Salt and pepper
4 eggs
¼ cup light cream

1. Cook spinach according to package directions. Drain thoroughly. Melt butter in a small skillet. Add onion and cook until soft but not browned. Toss onion and butter with spinach. Season with salt and pepper.

2. Butter two individual casseroles. Divide spinach between casseroles. Break 2 eggs on top of each spinach bed. Pour 1 tablespoon cream over each egg. Season.

3. Bake in a 350 degree oven until eggs are set to your liking.

Makes two servings.

EGGS BENEDICT

8 slices Canadian bacon
Water
1 teaspoon salt
3 tablespoons white vinegar
8 eggs
4 English muffins, sliced in half and
  toasted
Hollandaise sauce
Black olive slices
Parsley

1. Sauté the Canadian bacon just until heated through.

2. Fill a 12-inch skillet one inch deep with water. Add salt and vinegar and bring to a boil.

3. Break each egg carefully into a small bowl or saucer. Slide egg slowly into boiling water. Reduce heat. When eggs are firm (about 10 minutes) remove from water with a slotted spoon. Trim off ragged white edges.

4. Put a slice of cooked Canadian bacon on each half English muffin and top with one of the poached eggs. Cover with Hollandaise sauce. Garnish with olives and parsley.
    Makes four servings.

HOLLANDAISE SAUCE

3 egg yolks
1 tablespoon cold water
¼ teaspoon salt
½ teaspoon lemon juice
½ cup butter, melted

1. Combine egg yolks, water, salt, and lemon juice in blender. Switch on just long enough to mix.

2. As blender is running, add hot butter slowly until mixture thickens (about 20 seconds).

3. Serve immediately over eggs.
    Makes about two-thirds of a cup.

EXTRA RICH HOLLANDAISE

1 cup butter or margarine
4 egg yolks
2 tablespoons lemon juice
¼ teaspoon salt

¼ teaspoon white pepper
¼ teaspoon Tabasco sauce

1. Melt butter in a small saucepan until very hot but not brown.

2. Place egg yolks, lemon juice, salt, pepper, and Tabasco in blender. Cover and switch on just enough to blend.

3. Pour hot butter in a steady stream into yolks while they are blending.

4. Serve immediately.
Makes about one cup.

EGGS EN CROUTE
4 thick slices French or Italian bread
½ cup butter or margarine, melted
4 eggs
Salt and pepper
1 cup cheese or tomato sauce

1. Scoop a small hollow out of center of each bread slice and discard. Dip each slice in melted butter and place on baking sheet. Break an egg into each hollow. Sprinkle with salt and pepper.

2. Bake in a 325 degree oven until eggs are set. Serve with heated cheese or tomato sauce.
Makes four servings.

EGGS VEGETARIAN
1 package (10 ounces) frozen, creamed
    spinach, cooked according to
    directions
4 soft poached eggs
4 artichoke hearts
4 English muffins, split and toasted
Hollandaise sauce

1. Place spinach, eggs, and artichoke hearts on toasted English muffins. Top with Hollandaise sauce.
Makes four servings.

REUBEN SANDWICH

12 slices rye or pumpernickel bread
3 tablespoons prepared mustard
6 tablespoons sauerkraut
1 pound sliced corned beef
12 slices Swiss cheese
6 tablespoons butter or margarine

　　1. On each of 6 slices of bread, spread ½ tablespoon mustard; top with 1 tablespoon sauerkraut. Arrange slices of corned beef and 2 slices of Swiss cheese on each, then top with remaining pieces of bread.
　　2. Butter outside of each sandwich, using ½ tablespoon butter. Grill until cheese begins to melt.
　　Makes six sandwiches.

OYSTER POOR BOYS

¾ cup flour
¾ cup yellow cornmeal
2 teaspoons salt
½ teaspoon cayenne pepper, or to taste
½ teaspoon paprika
Fresh shelled oysters
Oil for frying
French bread or rolls
Lettuce
Mayonnaise or cocktail sauce

　　1. Combine flour, cornmeal, salt, cayenne, and paprika. Mix well.
　　2. Rinse oysters, drain, and pat dry. Roll oysters in cornmeal mixture. Let oysters stand for a few minutes before cooking.
　　3. Heat oil in a deep kettle or deep fat fryer. Fry a few oysters at a time for about two minutes or until golden brown.
　　4. Slice bread or rolls in half lengthwise. Place cooked oysters in bread with lettuce and either mayonnaise or cocktail sauce.

TUNA MELTS

1 can (6½ ounces) tuna packed
   in water
⅓ cup mayonnaise
½ medium apple, peeled and diced
1 stalk celery, finely chopped
1 scallion, finely chopped
½ teaspoon curry powder
Salt
Freshly ground black pepper
Butter
6 to 8 slices bread, toasted
1 cup Cheddar cheese, grated

1. Drain tuna. Put in a bowl and flake with a fork. Add mayonnaise, apple, celery, scallion, curry, salt, and pepper to taste. Mix well.

2. Butter toast if desired. Spread tuna mixture about one-half inch thick on toast. Top with grated cheese.

3. Put sandwiches on a baking sheet. Broil until cheese is hot and bubbly. Serve at once.

Makes six to eight servings.

TRIPLE THREATS

18 slices bread, buttered
12 slices baked ham
6 slices cooked chicken
6 thin slices Swiss cheese
3 eggs, slightly beaten
¼ cup milk
¼ teaspoon salt
Butter or margarine

1. Use 3 slices of bread for each sandwich. Cover first slice with a slice of ham and a slice of chicken. Top second slice of bread with ham and Swiss cheese. Cover with third slice of bread. Press slightly and hold together with toothpicks.

2. Trim crust. Cut in half diagonally.

3. Combine eggs, milk, and salt. Dip sandwich halves in egg mixture. Fry in butter until golden brown on both sides. Remove toothpicks. Serve, piping hot, with cranberry sauce or currant jelly.

Makes six sandwiches.

TRAINING CAMP WAFFLES

1¾ cups all-purpose flour
2 teaspoons double-acting
  baking powder
½ teaspoon salt
1 tablespoon sugar
3 eggs, separated
⅓ cup butter or margarine, melted
1½ cups milk

1. Sift together flour, baking powder, salt, and sugar into a mixing bowl. Set aside.

2. Beat egg yolks lightly. Add melted butter and milk and mix well. (If waffles are to be eaten soon, heat waffle iron and continue with batter. Otherwise, cover dry ingredients and egg-milk mixture and set aside until ready.)

3. Add egg mixture to dry ingredients and mix just until well blended. The batter should be slightly lumpy.

4. Beat egg whites until stiff but not dry. Gently fold into waffle batter mixture.

5. Bake waffles according to directions for your particular kind and size of waffle iron.

Makes about six waffles, depending on size of waffle iron.

Variations:

1. If waffles are to be served as a main dish with creamed chicken or ham, omit the sugar.

2. Cheese waffles: Omit the sugar and use 3 tablespoons butter and ½ cup grated Cheddar cheese.

3. Raisin or pecan waffles: Add ½ cup chopped, seedless raisins or ¾ cup finely diced pecans to waffle batter just before baking.

4. Fruit waffles: Add 1 more tablespoon sugar and 1 teaspoon freshly grated lemon or orange rind. Before folding in egg whites, fold in 1 cup blueberries, strawberries, or bananas.

5. Chocolate chip waffles: Add ¾ cup semi-sweet chocolate pieces to batter before baking.

WAFFLE TOPPERS

CINNAMON HONEY BUTTER
6 tablespoons butter
¼ teaspoon cinnamon
Freshly grated nutmeg
1 cup honey

    1. Melt butter in a small saucepan. Blend in cinnamon and a dash of nutmeg. Add honey and heat just to the boiling point. Serve warm.
    Makes one and one-third cups.

GOLDEN PEACH TOPPER
1 package (12 ounces) frozen peaches
¼ cup sugar
1 tablespoon cornstarch
¼ cup water

    1. Thaw peaches. Drain and reserve syrup. Chop peaches.
    2. Blend sugar and cornstarch in a saucepan. Stir in water, peaches, and peach syrup. Cook, stirring constantly, until mixture comes to a boil. Boil one minute. Serve warm.
    Makes one and one-third cups.

CINNAMON CREAM SYRUP
1 cup sugar
½ cup light corn syrup
½ teaspoon cinnamon
¼ cup water
½ cup evaporated milk

    1. In a small saucepan combine sugar, corn syrup, cinnamon, and water. Bring to a boil and cook two minutes, stirring constantly.
    2. Remove from heat and cool five minutes. Stir in evaporated milk. Serve warm.
    Makes one and two-thirds cups.

POTATO WAFFLES

1¼ cups all-purpose flour
¼ cup instant mashed potato granules
2 teaspoons sugar
2 teaspoons baking powder
½ teaspoon salt
3 eggs
⅓ cup salad oil
1½ cups milk

1. Sift together flour, potato granules, sugar, baking powder, and salt in a large bowl.

2. Beat eggs thoroughly. Add salad oil and milk. Combine liquid and dry ingredients and blend thoroughly.

3. Bake waffles according to directions for your particular kind and size of waffle iron.

Makes six to eight waffles.

NEW YORK YOGURT WAFFLES

1 cup all-purpose flour
1 teaspoon baking powder
¼ teaspoon salt
½ teaspoon baking soda
2 eggs, separated
2 tablespoons honey
1 cup plain yogurt
½ cup milk
2 tablespoons butter or margarine, melted

1. Sift together flour, baking powder, salt, and baking soda into a bowl. Set aside.

2. Beat egg yolks until thick. Beat in honey, yogurt, milk, and butter. Beat until smooth.

3. Add dry ingredients and mix well but do not over-beat.

4. Beat egg whites until stiff but not dry. Fold carefully into batter.

5. Bake waffles according to directions for your particular kind and size of waffle iron.

Makes six waffles.

CHOCOLATE WAFFLES

1½ cups sifted cake flour
2 teaspoons double-acting baking
  powder
½ teaspoon cinnamon
½ teaspoon nutmeg
½ cup butter or margarine
¾ cup sugar
2 eggs
1 teaspoon vanilla
2 squares semi-sweet chocolate, melted
  and cooled
½ cup milk
Whipped cream, ice cream, or chocolate curls

1. Sift together flour, baking powder, cinnamon, and nutmeg in a mixing bowl. Set aside.

2. Cream together butter and sugar until light. Add eggs, singly, and beat well after each addition.

3. Add vanilla and melted chocolate and blend well.

4. Add half the flour mixture and blend lightly. Stir in milk and add remaining flour mixture and beat just until blended.

5. Bake waffles according to directions for your particular kind and size of waffle iron.

6. Serve with whipped cream or ice cream and chocolate curls.

Makes six waffles.

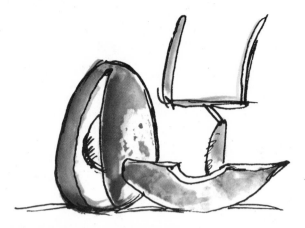

GAMETIME GAZPACHO

3 large ripe tomatoes, peeled, cored,
   and seeded
3 to 4 scallions, cut up
1 large stalk celery, chopped
Salt, to taste
Freshly ground black pepper
1 teaspoon dried dill weed
1 teaspoon wine vinegar
1 teaspoon olive oil
1 to 2 teaspoons Jalapeño sauce
   (optional)

   1. Place all ingredients in blender.
Blend until smooth.
   2. Chill well before serving. Serve
with a slice of lemon, if desired.
   Makes two to three servings.

GOAL LINE GUACAMOLE

2 ripe avocados, seeded and peeled
¼ cup onion, finely minced
4 teaspoons lime juice
1 small ripe tomato, peeled, seeded,
   and chopped
Jalapeño sauce (if desired)
Salt, to taste
Freshly ground pepper

   1. Cut avocados in chunks. Place in
blender. Add remaining ingredients.
Process until smooth and well blended.
   2. Chill. Serve with tortilla or corn
chips.
   Makes eight servings.

BRONCOS NACHOS

1 bag (16 ounces) tortilla chips
1 can (15 ounces) refried beans
1½ cups sharp Cheddar cheese, grated
Sliced Jalapeño peppers or diced green
   chiles, to taste

   1. Spread tortilla chips in a nine-
inch pie plate. Spread refried beans

over chips. Top with grated cheese and desired amount of peppers or chiles.

2. Broil about six inches from heat until cheese melts and mixture is piping hot.

CHALUPAS
Cooking oil
8 corn tortillas
1 pound lean ground beef
Salt
Freshly ground black pepper
Garlic powder
1 can (15 ounces) refried beans
¾ cup water
1 red onion, finely chopped
Shredded iceberg lettuce
4 ripe tomatoes, peeled and diced
2 cups Cheddar cheese, grated
Guacamole

1. Heat about ¼-inch cooking oil in a large skillet. Fry each tortilla in hot oil, about three seconds on each side or until soft and pliable. Set aside.

2. Cook beef in a skillet until cooked and lightly browned. Season with salt, pepper, and garlic powder.

3. Combine refried beans and water in a saucepan and heat, stirring occasionally.

4. Place a tortilla on a serving plate. Top with a layer of beans. Then top with cooked beef, a little chopped onion, lettuce, tomato, and grated cheese. Spoon guacamole on top. Serve at once.

Makes eight servings.

ENCHILADAS

2 pounds lean ground beef
1 large onion, chopped
Cooking oil
2 cans (7½ ounces each) enchilada
  sauce
12 corn tortillas
2 cups sharp Cheddar cheese, grated

1. Cook beef and onion in 1 table-spoon hot oil in a skillet until cooked and lightly browned. Stir in 1 can enchilada sauce. Set mixture aside.

2. Fill a large skillet with enough cooking oil to make it about one quarter-inch deep. Heat oil. Fry each tortilla in hot oil about three seconds on each side or just enough to be pliable.

3. Divide some of ½ of the meat mixture into each tortilla. Roll tortilla and place in a single layer in a flat casserole or baking dish.

4. Top with remaining half of the meat mixture, remaining can of enchilada sauce, and grated cheese.

5. Bake in a 350 degree oven 15 or 20 minutes or until mixture is hot and cheese is bubbly.

Makes 12 enchiladas.

CHILE CON QUESO

1 small onion, chopped
2 cloves garlic, finely minced
1 tablespoon oil
1 cup Cheddar cheese, grated
½ cup Monterey Jack cheese, diced
¼ cup cream
1 medium ripe tomato, peeled and
  chopped
1 can (7½ ounces) chopped green
  chiles
1 to 2 teaspoons Jalapeño sauce
  (optional)

1. Fry onion and garlic in hot oil until tender but not browned.

2. Add cheeses and cook over very low heat, stirring, until cheese melts. Add cream and stir constantly until well heated.

3. Stir in tomato, green chiles, and Jalapeño sauce, if desired. Heat, but do not boil.

4. Serve warm from the skillet with tortilla or corn chips.

Makes about two cups.

BEEF FONDUE

2½ pounds lean sirloin or other tender beef
Salad or peanut oil
Assorted sauces

1. Cut meat in three-quarter-inch cubes.

2. Fill a beef fondue pot with oil to about halfway and heat to the boiling point. Set pot over heating unit on serving table and place a small piece of bread in the bottom to prevent spattering.

3. Guests spear one cube of meat at a time on a fondue fork and cook it in the hot oil to suit their individual tastes. When meat is done, guests transfer meat from fondue forks to table forks and dip it in Bearnaise sauce, soy sauce mixed with ginger or garlic, a hot or mild curry sauce, or the sauce of their choice.

SAUCES FOR FONDUE

CLASSIC BERNAISE SAUCE

3 tablespoons white wine vinegar
¼ teaspoon black pepper
1 teaspoon tarragon, crumbled
1 teaspoon chives or green onions, minced
2 eggs, slightly beaten
2 tablespoons lemon juice
1 cup butter, melted and hot

1. Simmer white wine vinegar, pepper, tarragon, and chives or green onions in pot until liquid is reduced by half.

2. Place in blender with eggs and lemon juice. Blend a few seconds. Add butter and blend until smooth.

Note: Sauce can be made ahead and reheated slowly in top of double boiler or over pan of hot water before serving.

GENTLE CURRY SAUCE

1 small onion, chopped
1 small clove garlic, minced
1 piece (1-inch long) ginger root, slivered
1 tablespoon butter
½ tablespoon curry powder
½ teaspoon dark brown sugar
1½ tablespoons flour
¼ teaspoon salt
1 cup chicken stock

1. Sauté onion, garlic, and ginger in butter until onion is lightly browned. Stir in curry and sugar and cook one minute. Stir in flour and salt and cook one minute.

2. Gradually stir in chicken stock and cook, stirring, until sauce is smooth and thickened. Cook over low heat 10 minutes, stirring frequently.

3. Strain. Serve hot or cold.
Makes about one and a quarter cups sauce.

PHILADELPHIA GREEN SAUCE

1 slice white bread
¼ cup white vinegar
½ teaspoon anchovy paste
1 cup parsley, finely snipped
1½ teaspoons capers, chopped
2 cloves garlic, crushed
1½ teaspoons onion, grated
4 teaspoons olive oil
½ teaspoon sugar
2 tablespoons white vinegar

1. Remove crusts from bread and soak in ¼ cup white vinegar.

2. Combine with remaining ingredients, except 2 tablespoons white vinegar. Beat mixture to a smooth paste. Stir in more vinegar and more oil if desired.
Makes about one cup sauce.

FOOTBALL FONDUE I

1 garlic clove, peeled and split
2 cups dry white wine
½ cup Swiss cheese, shredded
½ pound Gruyere cheese, shredded
2 tablespoons flour
2 tablespoons kirsch or brandy (optional)
Dash nutmeg

Crusty 1-inch cubes of Italian or French
   bread, one side having crust
Sliced apples or pears
Cantaloupe or honeydew chunks

1. Rub the garlic clove around the inside of fondue pot. Add the wine and allow to simmer. <u>Do not boil.</u>

2. Sprinkle cheese with flour. Toss lightly. Gradually add to wine by handfuls when bubbles begin to rise to surface. Stir constantly until cheese has melted and mixture becomes smooth.

3. Add kirsch or brandy and seasonings, stirring constantly until well blended.

Makes six servings.

Note: For a milder fondue, substitute more Swiss cheese for the Gruyere. For a stronger flavor, substitute more Gruyere for the Swiss. Another version would be to substitute Cheddar for the Gruyere or Swiss. In this variation substitute cornstarch for the flour. If the cheese becomes too thick, add a little warm wine to the fondue to return the mixture to a thinner consistency. On the other hand, if the fondue begins to separate or become lumpy, combine 3 tablespoons warm white wine with 1 tablespoon cornstarch and add to mixture, stirring until smooth.

FOOTBALL FONDUE II
1 can or bottle (12 ounces) beer
2 teaspoons lemon juice
½ pound Swiss cheese, shredded
½ pound Gruyere cheese, shredded
2 tablespoons flour
¼ teaspoon garlic salt
½ teaspoon sweet-hot mustard
Cubed French or Italian bread with
   crust on one side

1. Pour beer and lemon juice into a fondue pot. Gradually heat on low temperature until just under boiling.

2. Toss cheese with flour, garlic salt, and mustard. Gradually add to the beer by the handfuls, stirring constantly after each addition to ensure melting of cheese. Continue stirring until smooth.

CHOCOLATE FONDUE
1 large (20 ounces) milk chocolate bar
1 cup heavy cream
2 tablespoons instant coffee powder
Angel food cake squares
Bananas in thick slices
Whole strawberries
Pineapple chunks

1. Break chocolate into one-inch squares and place in fondue pot. Add cream and instant coffee powder. Cook over very low heat, stirring, until chocolate is melted and mixture is smooth.

2. Place over very low heat, accompanied by a selection of foods to be dipped into the sauce and eaten for dessert.

HOT STUFFED AVOCADOS
2 tablespoons butter or margarine
2 tablespoons flour
1 cup light cream
½ teaspoon Worcestershire sauce
2 tablespoons onion, grated
2 tablespoons celery, finely chopped
2 cups cooked chicken, crab meat, or lobster
3 ripe avocados, peeled and halved
½ cup Cheddar cheese, grated

1. Melt butter in a saucepan. Add flour and cook one minute, stirring constantly. Stir in cream. Cook over low heat, stirring, until mixture comes to a boil and thickens.

2. Stir in Worcestershire sauce, onion, celery, and chicken or fish. Heat, but do not boil.

3. Place avocado halves in a baking dish. Fill with creamed mixture. Top with grated cheese.

4. Pour about ¼-inch water in bottom of baking dish. Bake at 350 degrees 15 to 20 minutes or just until avocados are hot and cheese is melted.

Makes six servings.

BALTIMORE BAKED SHRIMP
½ cup green onions, minced
¼ cup butter or margarine
½ pound Cheddar cheese, grated

34

½ teaspoon dry mustard
½ teaspoon salt
½ teaspoon garlic, minced
6 tablespoons sherry
1 pound cooked shrimp, peeled and
    deveined

1. Sauté onion in butter in a skillet just until onion is tender. Add cheese, dry mustard, salt, and garlic. Cook over very low heat, stirring constantly, until cheese is melted. Stir in sherry.

2. Place shrimp in a shallow broiler-proof baking dish. Pour cheese sauce over shrimp. Broil six inches from source of heat about five minutes or just until mixture is piping hot.

Makes four servings.

SAINTS BAKED STUFFED CRAB

½ pound French bread, sliced
½ cup celery, chopped
½ cup green onion, chopped (including
    tops)
1 clove garlic, minced
¼ cup butter or margarine
1 pound crab meat, picked over
2 tablespoons parsley, chopped
2 eggs, lightly beaten
Salt
Black pepper
Cayenne
Thyme
12 crab shells or ramekins, cleaned

1. Soak bread in enough water to cover. Squeeze water from bread. Set bread aside.

2. Sauté celery, onion, and garlic in hot butter over medium heat for about five minutes, stirring frequently.

3. Stir in soaked bread, crab meat, parsley, and eggs. Mix well. Season to taste with salt, pepper, cayenne, and thyme. Cook over low heat 15 minutes, stirring occasionally. Cool mixture.

4. Pile mixture into crab shells. Place on a baking sheet and bake in a 350 degree oven 15 to 20 minutes or until piping hot.

Makes six servings of two crab shells per serving.

COMMISSIONER'S POTATO PANCAKES

6 medium potatoes, peeled and grated
½ onion, finely minced
1 teaspoon salt
¼ teaspoon pepper
2 eggs, beaten
1 tablespoon flour
2 tablespoons parsley, chopped
   (optional)
¼ teaspoon nutmeg (optional)
Shortening

1. Combine all ingredients, except shortening, in a bowl and mix well.

2. Melt shortening in a skillet. Drop large spoonfuls of potato mixture into hot shortening and brown well on both sides.

3. Drain on paper towels. Serve hot.

BAKED STUFFED MUSHROOMS

1½ to 2 dozen large white mushrooms, (caps and stems), thoroughly cleaned
⅓ pound sliced bacon
3 tablespoons bacon fat
½ pound king crab meat
½ cup Cheddar or Swiss cheese, grated
½ cup Gruyere cheese, grated
⅓ cup dry bread crumbs

1. Snap off stems from mushroom caps. Set caps aside. Chop enough mushroom stems to make ¼ cup chopped stems. Reserve remaining stems for other uses.

2. Cook bacon until soft but not crisp. Drain bacon. Cut into small pieces. Combine bacon pieces with 3 tablespoons reserved bacon fat.

3. Combine bacon pieces with crab meat, Cheddar cheese, Gruyere cheese, bread crumbs, and mushroom stems.

4. Stuff mushroom caps with mixture. Place mushrooms on a baking pan.

5. Bake 15 minutes at 325 degrees or until piping hot.

LAZY MAN'S PIEROGI

1 package (8 ounces) egg noodles
½ cup butter or margarine
1 large onion, thinly sliced

1 can (10 ounces) sauerkraut, well
   drained

1. Cook noodles according to package directions. Drain.
2. Melt butter in a large saucepan. Add onion and cook just until tender but not browned. Add sauerkraut and heat thoroughly.
3. Add noodles and cook just until heated through.
Makes four servings.

FETTUCINE DI BAFFI
1 pound fettucine
½ cup cream, warmed
¼ cup butter, melted
2 to 4 tablespoons Romano or Parmesan
   cheese, grated
¼ cup ricotta cheese
1 egg, lightly beaten
Parsley, chopped (optional)

1. Cook fettucine in boiling salted water to which a dash of oil has been added.

2. When fettucine has been cooked "al dente," firm and a bit sticky on the teeth, drain quickly and place in a large, warm mixing or serving bowl.
3. Add remaining ingredients. Toss quickly and serve at once with more grated Parmesan cheese and chopped parsley, if desired.
Makes four to six servings.

FETTUCINE ALFREDO
2 pounds fettucine
½ pound butter
2 cups Parmesan cheese, freshly grated

1. Cook the fettucine in boiling salted water until tender but still firm. Drain.
2. Cut the butter in small pieces and put in a deep, heated serving dish. Add the hot fettucine and sprinkle with the cheese. Using a fork and spoon, quickly toss the fettucine until well coated with butter and cheese. Serve at once.
Makes eight servings.

BART STARR'S FAVORITE SALAD

3 cups salad oil
1 cup cider or wine vinegar
¼ cup Worcestershire sauce
¼ cup Parmesan cheese, grated
1 teaspoon Italian seasoning
3 cloves garlic, finely minced
Salt
Freshly ground black pepper
1 head iceberg or Romaine lettuce
½ unpeeled cucumber, sliced
½ red onion, sliced
6 to 8 cherry tomatoes, halved
1 stalk celery, diced
8 to 10 black olives, cut up
½ avocado, diced
½ cup Fontina or hard white cheese,
   grated
½ cup seasoned croutons

1. Combine salad oil, vinegar, Worcestershire sauce, Parmesan cheese, Italian seasoning, garlic, salt, and pepper to taste in a container. Cover and let stand several hours, or overnight.

2. Combine lettuce, cucumber, onion, tomatoes, celery, olives, avocado, cheese, and croutons in a salad bowl.

3. Add desired amount of dressing and toss lightly.

Makes six servings of salad and about one quart salad dressing.

SICILIAN SALAD

Ripe tomato slices
Red onion slices
Cucumber slices, peeled
Wine vinegar
Olive oil
Salt
Freshly ground black pepper
Oregano

1. Arrange tomato, onion, and cucumber slices on individual salad plates or salad bowls.

2. Combine vinegar and oil in the proportion of ¾ vinegar to ¼ oil. Add salt and pepper to taste.

3. Pour dressing over salad in desired amount. Sprinkle with oregano to taste.

SWEETWATER BLACK BOTTOM PIE

1 nine-inch frozen pie shell
1 package (6 ounces) semi-sweet
  chocolate pieces
¼ cup white corn syrup
1 package (3½ ounces) vanilla
  pudding and pie mix
1 cup milk
2 cups heavy cream
½ teaspoon vanilla
¾ cup dark rum
Whipped cream
Chocolate curls

1. Bake pie shell according to package directions. Cool.

2. Melt chocolate in a pan over hot water. Add corn syrup and stir until blended. Cool slightly. Pour into pie shell.

3. Cook pudding mix according to package directions using only 1 cup milk. Remove from heat and cool, stirring to avoid skin forming on top. Chill.

4. Whip cream until stiff but not dry. Add pudding, vanilla, and rum. Mix lightly but thoroughly. Pour over chocolate in pie shell.

5. Refrigerate at least one hour. Garnish with additional whipped cream and chocolate curls before serving.

Makes 8 to 10 servings.

ST. LOUIS SOUR CREAM PIE

2 eggs
1 cup dairy sour cream
1 cup seedless raisins
⅔ cup sugar
1½ teaspoons cinnamon
¼ teaspoon salt
¾ cup pecans
1 9-inch unbaked pastry shell

1. Preheat oven to 400 degrees.

2. Combine eggs, sour cream, raisins, sugar, cinnamon, and salt in blender. Cover and process until blended. Add pecans and chop briefly. Pour mixture into unbaked shell.

3. Bake 15 minutes. Lower oven temperature to 350 degrees and bake 30 minutes longer or until a knife inserted in center of pie comes out clean.

Makes six to eight servings.

HALFTIME RAISIN-APPLE PIE

4 or 5 tart cooking apples
¾ cup sugar
2 tablespoons whole wheat flour
½ teaspoon cinnamon
½ teaspoon nutmeg
¾ cup seedless raisins
¾ cup seedless golden raisins
2 nine-inch frozen deep-dish pie crusts
1 can (1 pound) pear halves
2 to 3 tablespoons rum or brandy
3 tablespoons butter or margarine,
    melted
⅓ cup black walnuts, finely chopped

1. Core and pare apples. Cut into thin slices. Place in a mixing bowl with sugar, flour, cinnamon, and nutmeg. Mix well.

2. Cover raisins with boiling water. Let stand five minutes. Drain. Add to apple mixture. Cover and refrigerate 30 minutes.

3. Defrost pie crusts. Place one crust carefully in a nine-inch pie pan.

4. Drain pear halves well. Crush pears with a fork.

5. Arrange ⅓ of the apple mixture in pie crust. Top with ½ of pear mixture, 1 tablespoon rum, and 1 tablespoon melted butter.

6. Repeat layers. Sprinkle walnuts on top.

7. Cover with second pie crust. Crimp edges with fingers. Prick center several times with a fork.

8. Bake in a 425 degree oven 45 to 50 minutes or until top is lightly browned and filling is bubbly.

CHEERLEADER CHEESE CAKE

2 cups vanilla wafer crumbs
½ cup butter or margarine, melted
⅓ cup and ½ cup sugar
1 package (8 ounces) cream cheese
½ cup dairy sour cream
1 tablespoon lemon juice
1 teaspoon vanilla
½ cup dairy whipped topping

1. Combine vanilla wafer crumbs, butter, and ⅓ cup sugar. Pour into an eight-inch pie plate. Press mixture down with the hand or back of spoon to form a crust on bottom and sides of pie plate. Bake in a 350 degree oven 15 minutes or until set and lightly browned. Cool.

2. Beat cream cheese until fluffy. Add ½ cup sugar gradually. Blend in sour cream, lemon juice, vanilla, and whipped topping.

3. Pour into baked crust. Chill at least two hours in refrigerator before serving.

Makes six servings.

CANOLI DI BAFFI

1 pound ricotta cheese
½ cup confectioners' sugar
½ teaspoon vanilla
1 chocolate bar with almonds, chopped, or ½ cup chopped candied fruit, or ½ cup chopped pistachio nuts
8 to 10 canoli shells

1. Put cheese in bowl of electric mixer. Beat at high speed until smooth (three to four minutes).

2. Add sugar and vanilla and beat three to four minutes.

3. Fold ¾ of the chocolate into blended cheese. Stuff canoli shells with mixture. Sprinkle remaining chocolate on ends of canoli. Dust tops with confectioners' sugar.

Makes 8 to 10 servings.

Note: Canoli shells are not easy to make, so we suggest buying them from an Italian bakery or delicatessen.

TAILGATE PARTIES
FROM PARKING LOT PICNICS TO OUTDOOR BANQUETS

Years ago, some enterprising football fans found that the tailgate of a station wagon made an ideal table for a pre-game meal.

Now, come rain or shine, heat or snow, stadium parking lots are filled with vehicles of all sizes and types, from pick-up trucks to palatial motor homes, their occupants enjoying "tailgate" meals ranging from the most basic to the ultra-extravagant.

A basic tailgate picnic basket should have the appropriate allotment of plates (if paper, the heavy, coated type is best for food that has to be cut or is apt to run), knives, forks, spoons, glasses (plastic or crystal depending on how fancy you wish to be), plus a tablecloth (or blanket) and napkins, corkscrew, can opener, bread knife, small wooden board (for cutting bread, meat, or cheese), a carving knife, salt and pepper shakers, paper towels, and, if you're so inclined, candles (don't forget the matches!).

Take wine or beer, and tea or coffee in a Thermos. A couple of wide-mouth jugs are just the thing for soups, stews, and chilis. If you have soup you also may want to include several heavy mugs.

A cooler—big or small depending on the size of your party—is another necessity. It will do the obvious—keep cold food cold until serving time in addition to holding a supply of ice and drinks. It also will keep hot foods hot if they are packed carefully. On the other hand, a casserole, soup pot, or stew dish wrapped in several layers of newspaper and packed in a cardboard box will keep hot for several hours.

Whatever your menu and dining style, a tailgate picnic is great fun, especially on a crisp fall day with the excitement of the game in the air.

MUSHROOM STUFFED EGGS

6 hard-cooked eggs
¼ cup fresh mushrooms, minced
1 tablespoon mayonnaise
1 teaspoon Dijon mustard
Salt and pepper
Dash cayenne pepper

1. Halve the eggs lengthwise. Remove yolks and mash in a bowl with mushrooms, mayonnaise, mustard, salt and pepper to taste, and cayenne pepper.
2. Stuff mixture into the egg whites. Pack closely together, upright in a plastic container. Chill.
Makes 12 egg halves.

CHICKEN LIVER PÂTÉ

1 pound chicken livers
½ cup dry white wine
¾ cup chicken broth
1 sprig parsley
¼ cup onion, finely minced
¼ teaspoon ground ginger
1 tablespoon soy sauce
½ cup butter or margarine, softened
¾ teaspoon salt
¼ teaspoon dry mustard
1 tablespoon brandy

1. Simmer chicken livers with wine, broth, parsley, onion, ginger, and soy sauce until tender. Cool in liquid.
2. Remove livers and place in blender. Add butter, salt, mustard, and brandy. Blend until very smooth. If mixture is too stiff, add a little of the cooking liquid.
3. Press mixture into a crock with a tight cover. Refrigerate.
Makes two cups.

ALL-PRO PÂTÉ

1 pound ground lean pork
1 pound ground veal
½ cup onion, finely chopped
½ cup parsley, snipped
1½ teaspoons salt
½ teaspoon ground black pepper
1 tablespoon Worcestershire sauce
1 teaspoon basil leaves

2 tablespoons dry sherry
4 eggs, lightly beaten
Small sour pickles

1. Preheat oven to 375 degrees.
2. Place all ingredients, except pickles, in a large mixing bowl. Blend thoroughly with hands.
3. Turn mixture into an ungreased 9 x 5-inch loaf pan.
4. Bake one hour or until loaf is set.
5. Cool in baking pan. Turn out of pan, wrap in aluminum foil, and refrigerate.
6. Cut in thin slices and serve with small sour pickles as an appetizer or first course.
Makes 12 to 16 slices.

DALLAS DRUMSTICKS

12 chicken drumsticks
1 teaspoon salt
⅛ teaspoon pepper
½ cup saltine cracker crumbs
½ cup Parmesan cheese, grated
2 teaspoons chives, finely snipped
½ cup melted butter or margarine

1. Sprinkle drumsticks with salt and pepper. Combine crumbs, cheese, and chives. Dip chicken in butter, then roll in crumb mixture to coat well. Place in a flat baking pan lined with aluminum foil. Drizzle remaining butter over chicken.
2. Bake in a 375 degree oven 45 to 50 minutes or until browned and cooked.
3. Wrap pan in several layers of newspapers to take to tailgate picnic warm, or chill thoroughly, then pack in plastic bags and keep cold.
Makes six servings.

CURRIED CHICKEN DRUMSTICKS

½ cup fine dry bread crumbs
2 teaspoons onion powder
2 teaspoons curry powder
½ teaspoon salt
½ teaspoon dry mustard
1 clove garlic, peeled and minced
2½ pounds chicken drumsticks
1 cup milk

1. In a bowl combine bread crumbs, onion powder, curry powder, salt, mustard, and garlic. Blend well.

2. Dip the chicken drumsticks in milk and then in the crumb mixture. Place in a lightly greased shallow baking pan.

3. Bake in a 375 degree oven 45 minutes to one hour or until drumsticks are cooked. Turn once during baking.

4. These can be carried warm in the baking pan or packed chilled in plastic bags.

Makes 8 to 10 servings.

JETS MANHATTAN CLAM CHOWDER

¼ pound salt pork, cut in cubes, or 8
   slices bacon, cut up
2 small onions, finely chopped
½ green pepper, finely chopped
½ cup celery, chopped
6 medium potatoes, peeled and diced
3 cans (7 ounces each) minced clams
   with liquid
1 teaspoon pepper
1 teaspoon thyme
Dash cayenne pepper
4 cups water
3 cups tomato juice

1. In a Dutch oven cook pork or bacon until lightly browned and crisp. Add onions, green pepper, and celery. Cook slowly about five minutes, until tender but not browned.

2. Add potatoes. Barely cover with water. Bring to a boil, then reduce heat and simmer until potatoes are tender.

3. Add clams and juice, seasonings, and water. Heat to boiling. Reduce heat. Add tomato juice and heat thoroughly.

Makes six to eight servings.

PATRIOTS NEW ENGLAND CHOWDER

½ cup butter or margarine
4 large onions, finely chopped
3 large celery stalks, sliced
2 bay leaves
2 cans (8 ounces each) whole
   mushrooms with liquid
4 cans (14 ounces each) chicken broth
1½ cups dry white wine
1 pound large unshelled shrimp
3 frozen spiny lobsters, thawed and split
   in half
2 Dungeness crabs, cooked or frozen,
   thawed, cleaned, and cracked
2 pounds skinned, boned halibut or
   rockfish, cut into large chunks
6 to 8 medium-sized sole filets
3 cups heavy cream
¼ cup parsley, chopped

1. Melt butter in a large (three-gallon) kettle. Add onions, celery, and bay leaves. Simmer until vegetables are soft but not browned.

2. Add mushrooms with liquid, broth, and wine. Cover and bring to a boil.

3. Devein shrimp by slipping a metal or wooden skewer into the back of each shrimp just below the vein. Pull up through the shell to bring out the vein.

4. Add shrimp, lobster, and crab to stock in pot and cook 10 minutes.

5. Add halibut and sole. Cover and simmer six to eight minutes or just until fish is cooked. Remove from heat. Add cream. Cover and allow to stand several minutes.

6. Heat over very low heat, but do not boil. Serve topped with parsley.

Makes 8 to 10 servings.

47

MUSHROOM BARLEY SOUP

3 cups mushrooms, sliced
1 clove garlic, minced
½ cup onion, chopped
½ cup green pepper, chopped
⅓ cup butter or margarine
⅓ cup flour
3 cups chicken bouillon
2 cups milk
½ cup quick-cooking barley
2 teaspoons Worcestershire sauce
1 teaspoon dried parsley flakes
1½ teaspoons salt
Grind of fresh pepper
Pinch of paprika

1. In a five- or six-quart kettle sauté mushrooms, garlic, onion, and green pepper in butter just until onion is tender but not browned.

2. Add flour and cook over medium heat about three to four minutes or until flour is browned. Stir in bouillon, milk, barley, Worcestershire sauce, parsley, salt, pepper, and paprika.

3. Bring to a boil over medium heat, stirring often. Reduce heat, cover, and simmer 15 minutes or until barley is tender. Stir occasionally.

4. If soup is too thick, add a small amount of milk to give it the desired consistency.

Makes six servings.

VIKINGS VEGETABLE SOUP

1½ pounds beef soup meat
1 beef marrow bone
2 quarts water
4 teaspoons salt
2 teaspoons seasoned salt
¼ teaspoon pepper
4 celery stalks with leaves, sliced
8 carrots, peeled and cut in ½-inch slices
6 potatoes, peeled and diced
2 medium onions, thinly sliced
2 cans (1 pound each) tomatoes

1. Place soup meat, bone, water, salt, seasoned salt, pepper, and celery in a large soup pot or Dutch oven. Bring to a boil. Lower heat, cover, and simmer about one and a half hours. During first 30 minutes of cooking, skim top with a metal spoon.

2. Add carrots, potatoes, and onions. Simmer 30 minutes.

3. Remove meat and bone from soup. Cut meat into cubes and return to soup. Remove marrow from bone and return to soup.

4. Add tomatoes. Cover and continue simmering 20 to 30 minutes.

5. Taste and adjust seasonings. Makes about 12 servings.

WARMUP BEEF SOUP

3 to 4 pounds beef shank cross cuts, cut 1-inch thick
1 teaspoon salt
9 cups water
2 envelopes (1¼ ounces each) onion soup mix
¾ cup quick-cooking barley
10 whole peppercorns, tied in a square of cheesecloth
2 cups carrots, thinly sliced
2 cups celery, thinly sliced

1. Place beef in a large Dutch oven or soup kettle. Add salt and water. Cover tightly and simmer one and a half hours.

2. Add soup mix and continue cooking 40 minutes.

3. Add barley, peppercorns, carrots, and celery and cook 30 to 40 minutes or until meat and vegetables are cooked. (Remove peppercorns before taking to the tailgate party.)

Makes eight servings.

OAKLAND ONION SOUP

1½ pounds onions
¼ cup butter or margarine
2 tablespoons salad oil
1 teaspoon salt
Pinch of sugar
2 tablespoons flour
2 quarts canned beef bouillon
½ cup dry white wine or dry white
   vermouth
French bread
Swiss or Parmesan cheese, grated

1. Peel and cut onions into very thin slices. Melt butter and oil in a large saucepan or heavy Dutch oven. Add onions and simmer over low heat about 15 minutes.

2. Sprinkle salt and sugar over onions. Raise heat to moderate and cook about 30 minutes, stirring occasionally, until onions are tender and have turned an even golden brown.

3. Sprinkle flour over top of onions and stir and cook for two minutes.

4. Stir in beef bouillon and wine. Taste and add salt and pepper, if necessary. Simmer 30 to 40 minutes.

5. Serve with French bread, plain or toasted, and a generous dusting of cheese.

Makes six to eight servings.

MARINATED VEGETABLES

1 head cauliflower
1 bunch broccoli
½ pound mushrooms, cleaned
9 to 12 cherry tomatoes
1 bottle (16 ounces) Italian dressing

1. Break cauliflower into flowerettes. Peel broccoli stems and cut into slices; cut tops into small sections.

2. Place cauliflower and broccoli in a plastic bowl with a tight-fitting cover.

3. Add mushrooms and tomatoes. Pour dressing over top. Cover tightly.

4. Marinate several hours, turning bowl upside down occasionally.

5. Take plastic container to a tailgate picnic. The dressing can be drained at the picnic and used on a tossed green salad.

RATATOUILLE

2 cloves garlic, minced
1 onion, thinly sliced
½ cup olive oil
1 medium eggplant, peeled and diced
3 medium zucchini, thinly sliced
1 green pepper, seeded and sliced
1 can (28 ounces) Italian-style tomatoes
1 teaspoon oregano
Salt and pepper to taste

1. Cook garlic and onion in hot olive oil until tender but not browned. Add eggplant, zucchini, and green pepper and simmer 10 minutes. Add remaining ingredients. Cover and simmer 30 minutes.

2. Remove cover and simmer 30 minutes more, stirring occasionally.

3. Chill thoroughly.
Makes six to eight servings.

TABULI (CRACKED WHEAT SALAD)

1 cup bulgar (cracked wheat)
1 cucumber, peeled and finely diced
2 tomatoes, peeled and chopped
3 tablespoons green peppers, chopped
½ cup parsley, chopped
¼ cup fresh mint, chopped,
   or 1½ teaspoons dried mint leaves
½ cup scallions, chopped
½ cup olive oil
½ cup lemon juice
Salt

1. Wash the cracked wheat under cold water until it runs clear. Put in a bowl and cover with 8 cups boiling water. Let stand one to two hours. Rinse with cold water and drain well, squeezing out the excess water with your hands.

2. Put in a large bowl and add cucumber, tomatoes, green peppers, parsley, mint, and scallions. In a small bowl combine olive oil, lemon juice, and salt to taste.

3. Pour dressing over wheat mixture and toss well.

4. Put salad in a plastic container and chill until ready to take to a tailgate party.

Makes 8 to 10 servings.

SUPERBOIL POTATO SALAD

5 pounds new potatoes
6 hard-cooked eggs, finely chopped
12 stalks celery, finely chopped
2 tablespoons parsley, minced
2 medium onions, finely chopped
1 tablespoon yellow mustard
2 cups mayonnaise
Salt
Pepper

1. Wash potatoes. Place in a large saucepan with enough water to cover. Cook 15 to 20 minutes or until potatoes are tender but not overcooked. (If potatoes vary in size, remove smaller potatoes first to prevent overcooking.)

2. Drain potatoes and let stand until cool enough to handle. Peel and cut in ½-inch cubes. Place in a large mixing bowl.

3. Add eggs, celery, parsley, and onions and toss lightly. Combine mustard, mayonnaise, salt, and pepper to taste. Add to potatoes and toss lightly.

Makes 8 to 10 servings.

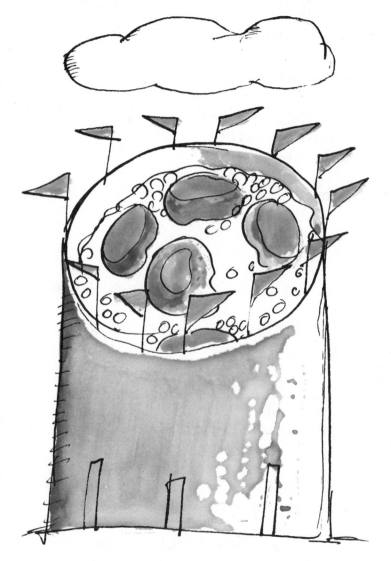

DENVER CHICKEN SALAD

4 cups cooked chicken, diced
½ cup almonds, chopped
2 cups celery, diced
Juice of 1 large lemon
1½ cups mayonnaise
½ pound bacon, fried crisp and
    crumbled
Lettuce cups

1. Combine all ingredients, except lettuce. Chill.
2. Line a serving dish with lettuce cups. Fill with chicken salad. For a tail-gate picnic, be certain that salad is well chilled and stays chilled.

SALAD NIÇOISE

3 cups cooked fresh green beans,
    chilled
6 tomatoes, peeled and quartered
French dressing
½ cup dry white wine
3 cups new potatoes, cooked, peeled,
    and sliced
1 can (12 ounces) tuna
Drained capers (optional)
Salad greens
½ cup small, pitted ripe olives
1 can (2 ounces) anchovy fillets
    (optional)

1. Combine green beans and tomatoes in a large plastic container. Cover with French dressing. Cover tightly and refrigerate several hours.
2. Heat wine. Pour over potato slices. Let stand at room temperature one hour. Refrigerate.
3. Pack beans, potatoes, and remaining ingredients in an insulated picnic container.
4. At the football game, open tuna, drain and place in center of a large wooden bowl or extra large paper platter. Mount potatoes at one side and sprinkle with capers. Surround with salad greens. Drain beans and tomatoes and place on greens. Garnish with olives and anchovy fillets.
5. Let everyone help themselves and serve with French bread, sliced and spread with sweet butter.

EAGLES WEDGE SALAD

1 pound fresh spinach, cleaned and cut
　　into bite-size pieces
1 teaspoon sugar
Salt
Pepper
6 hard-cooked eggs, sliced
½ pound boiled ham, cut into julienne
　　strips
½ head lettuce, shredded
1 package (10 ounces) frozen peas,
　　uncooked
1 Bermuda onion, thinly sliced
1 cup dairy sour cream
2 cups mayonnaise
½ pound Swiss cheese, cut into julienne
　　strips
½ pound bacon, crisply cooked

1. Spread spinach over bottom of
a large glass bowl. Sprinkle with a half
teaspoon sugar. Season with salt and
pepper to taste.

2. Layer eggs over spinach. Add
ham over top of eggs.

3. Add a layer of lettuce and sprinkle remaining sugar over top. Season to
taste with salt and pepper.

4. Scatter peas over top of lettuce.

5. Layer onion slices on lettuce.

6. Combine sour cream and mayonnaise and spread over top of layers.
Arrange cheese strips over top of
mayonnaise.

7. Cover bowl with plastic wrap and
refrigerate overnight.

8. At the tailgate picnic, sprinkle
bacon over top of salad. Do not toss, but
cut into wedges all the way through like
a pie.

Makes 10 servings.

QUARTERBACK GUMBO

½ cup shortening
½ cup flour
2 cups okra, chopped
1 large onion, chopped
⅔ cup celery, chopped
4 cloves garlic, minced
⅔ cup green pepper, chopped
2 cups cleaned fresh shrimp
1 cup crab meat
2 quarts hot water

54

2 teaspoons salt
¼ teaspoon red pepper sauce
1 teaspoon Worcestershire sauce
2 tablespoons catsup
Hot cooked rice

1. Melt shortening in a heavy saucepan or Dutch oven. Add flour and cook, stirring until flour turns brown. Add okra and sauté until okra ceases to rope.

2. Add onion, celery, garlic, and green pepper. Simmer over medium heat about 10 minutes, stirring often.

3. Add shrimp and crab meat. Simmer until shrimp turns pink (about 15 minutes).

4. Add water, salt, red pepper sauce, Worcestershire sauce, and catsup. Cover and simmer over low heat about one and a half hours. Serve over hot cooked rice.

Makes six to eight servings.

SUSIE MORTON'S EGGPLANT CASSEROLE *

1 medium eggplant
3 to 4 ripe tomatoes, thinly sliced
2 onions, thinly sliced
½ can (10 ounces) cheddar cheese soup
2 tablespoons light cream
Garlic salt
Freshly ground black pepper
1 cup Cheddar cheese, grated

1. Peel eggplant. Cut into ½-inch cubes. Soak in salt water 15 minutes. Drain. Cook in a small amount of boiling water until not quite tender.

2. Put drained eggplant in a casserole or baking dish. Cover with tomato slices and onion slices. Combine soup and cream and pour over top. Season with garlic salt and pepper. Sprinkle cheese over top of casserole.

3. Bake in a 350 degree oven 20 to 30 minutes or until casserole is piping hot and cheese is bubbly.

*Susie Morton is the wife of Denver Broncos quarterback Craig Morton.

BEARS MOUSSAKA

1 large eggplant
Oil for frying
4 medium onions, sliced
2 cloves garlic, minced
½ pound lean ground lamb
2 cans (8 ounces each) tomato sauce
1½ teaspoons salt
1 teaspoon oregano
2 tablespoons butter or margarine
2 tablespoons flour
¼ teaspoon nutmeg
1½ cups milk
2 egg yolks, beaten

1. Slice eggplant, without peeling, into ¼- to ½-inch thick slices.

2. Heat oil in a skillet over medium-high heat. Sauté eggplant slices until lightly browned on both sides. Drain on paper towels.

3. Place onions, garlic, and lamb in a skillet. Cook over medium-high heat, stirring occasionally, until lamb is lightly browned and onions are limp. Drain off as much accumulated fat as possible.

4. Add tomato sauce, salt, and oregano. Lower heat, cover, and simmer 20 minutes.

5. Melt butter in a small saucepan. Stir in flour, salt, and nutmeg, and cook 30 seconds. Remove from heat and add milk. Cook, stirring constantly, until mixture comes to a boil and is smooth and thick. Stir a small amount of the hot mixture into beaten egg yolks. Return to mixture in pan and stir well. Cook for one minute, stirring constantly.

6. Place a layer of eggplant on the bottom of a two-quart casserole. Top with a layer of lamb-tomato mixture. Repeat process until all of eggplant and lamb are used. Pour cream sauce over the top.

7. Bake in a 350 degree oven one hour or until mixture is hot and bubbly.

Makes four to six servings.

LASAGNA MALAVASI

2 tablespoons salad oil or olive oil
1 pound lean ground beef
1 pound ground veal
1 large onion, chopped
2 cloves garlic, minced
1 teaspoon basil
1 teaspoon oregano
2 teaspoons salt
1 can (30 ounces) peeled Italian
   tomatoes
1 can (6 ounces) tomato paste
¾ cup dry red wine
1 pound Italian sausage
½ pound lasagna noodles
½ pound ricotta cheese
1 pound mozzarella cheese, sliced
1 cup grated Parmesan and Romano
   cheese, mixed

1. Heat salad oil in a skillet over medium-high flame. Add beef and veal and cook until meat has lost its red color. Add onion and garlic and cook until onion is transparent. Add basil, oregano, salt, tomatoes, tomato paste, and red wine. Cover and simmer 30 minutes.

Remove cover and simmer an additional 30 minutes.

2. Fry sausage until cooked. Slice in thin slices and add to sauce.

3. Cook noodles until tender. Drain immediately.

4. Spoon a small amount of sauce in bottom of a 13 x 9 x 3-inch baking dish. Cover sauce with a layer of noodles. Cover noodles with a thin layer of ricotta, several slices of Mozzarella, and a liberal sprinkling of Parmesan cheese. Top with a layer of sauce.

5. Repeat process until all ingredients are used. End the process with a layer of Mozzarella cheese and Parmesan cheese.

6. Bake in a 350 degree oven 45 to 50 minutes or until hot and bubbly and the cheese is melted.

Makes six to eight servings.

WILD RICE AND TURKEY CASSEROLE

1 cup uncooked wild rice
¼ cup butter or margarine
4 stalks celery, chopped
1 can (8 ounces) chopped mushrooms
   or 1 pound fresh mushrooms, chopped
¼ small onion, chopped
4 cups turkey chunks, diced (use a
   frozen turkey roast or a fresh turkey
   breast)
3 tablespoons soy sauce
1 can (10¾ ounces) cream of mushroom
   soup
¾ cup water

　　1. Cook rice according to package directions.
　　2. Melt butter in a large skillet. Add celery, mushrooms, onion, and turkey. Cook, stirring constantly, for about five minutes
　　3. Add rice, soy sauce, soup, and water. Stir to mix.
　　4. Turn mixture into a two-quart casserole. Cover and bake in a 350 degree oven two hours.
　　Makes six to eight servings.

TAMPA BAY SKEWERED STEAK

1½ pounds flank steak
⅓ cup soy sauce
⅓ cup dark or light rum
Cherry tomatoes (optional)
2 tablespoons salad oil

　　1. Trim excess fat from steak. Wipe steak with damp paper towels. Cut steak into very thin strips. Set aside.
　　2. Combine soy sauce and rum in a bowl. Add steak pieces and toss to coat. Cover and refrigerate at least 24 hours.
　　3. Slide pieces of steak onto skewers, alternating with tomatoes, if desired. Brush lightly with oil. Grill over hot coals about one minute on each side, or to desired degree of doneness.
　　Makes about 30 skewers.

SAN FRANCISCO SHRIMP RUMAKI

1½ pounds raw shrimp, peeled and deveined
1 bottle (5 ounces) chili sauce
1 garlic clove, minced
12 slices bacon, partially cooked, but still soft

1. In a small bowl combine shrimp, chili sauce, and garlic. Refrigerate several hours.

2. Cut bacon slices in half. Wrap each shrimp in a half slice of bacon. Secure with toothpick.

3. Broil, or cook on a hibachi, several minutes on each side or until evenly browned and bacon is crisp.

Makes two dozen.

ARTICHOKE RUMAKI

1 package (9 ounces) frozen artichoke hearts
Onion or garlic salt
12 slices bacon, partially cooked

1. Cook artichoke hearts according to package directions. Drain well.

2. Sprinkle with onion or garlic salt. Cut bacon slices in half. Wrap each artichoke heart in a half slice of bacon. Secure with toothpick.

3. Broil, or cook on a hibachi, several minutes on each side or until evenly browned and bacon is crisp.

Makes two dozen.

INDONESIAN SATÉS

3 whole chicken breasts, skinned and
   boned
1 cup coconut milk
1 garlic clove, crushed
2 teaspoons coriander, crushed
1 teaspoon salt
½ teaspoon freshly ground pepper
½ cup creamy peanut butter
½ cup chicken broth
1 tablespoon chili powder
Dash cayenne pepper or liquid hot
   pepper seasoning

1. Cut chicken breasts into 1-inch cubes.

2. Combine coconut milk, garlic, coriander, salt, and pepper in a bowl; blend well. Add chicken pieces, stir to coat. Cover and refrigerate 24 hours.

3. In a bowl combine peanut butter, chicken broth, chili powder, and cayenne pepper. Blend until smooth.

4. Skewer chicken on bamboo sticks, three or four pieces to each stick. Grill over hot coals until brown but not dry, about three to four minutes on each side. Serve with peanut butter sauce.

Note: Canned coconut milk or coconut cream is available in the gourmet sections of most grocery stores. You can also make your own coconut milk. Take 2 cups grated unsweetened coconut and cover with 1 cup boiling water. Either put in a blender for 20 seconds or let stand 20 minutes. Pour through a fine strainer of double cheese cloth, squeezing coconut until no juice remains. Discard pulp. Add pinch of salt to coconut milk and use in recipe.

GRILL VARIATIONS

HIBACHI-STYLE VEGETABLES

1. Steam or cook carrots until just crisply tender. Dip in butter, thread on skewers, and heat on grill.

2. Cook frozen artichoke hearts as directed. Drain well. Marinate in French dressing. Thread on skewers and heat thoroughly.

3. Try these, too: cucumber chunks, mushrooms, green and red pepper slices, and cherry tomatoes. Marinate

for several hours in French dressing. Thread on skewers and cook three to four minutes on grill, turning once.

HIBACHI-STYLE FRUITS
1. Peel and halve bananas. Wrap with bacon and grill on both sides until bacon is crisp. Fresh figs, pineapple chunks, or dates are delicious alternatives.

2. Almost any fruit grills well with a brush of melted butter and a dash of cinnamon or ginger.

TAMALE PIES
1 medium onion, chopped
1 medium green pepper, seeded and chopped
1 clove garlic, minced
2 tablespoons salad oil
1 pound lean ground beef
2 cans (8 ounces each) tomato sauce
1 can (12 ounces) whole kernel corn
¼ cup dry red wine
1 teaspoon salt
¼ teaspoon pepper
1½ tablespoons chili powder, or to taste
1 package (12 ounces) corn bread mix
1 cup Cheddar cheese, grated
1 cup corn chips, crushed

1. Cook onion, green pepper, and garlic in oil in a large skillet until onion is tender but not browned. Add beef and cook, stirring with a fork, until meat is broken up and no longer red. Pour off excess drippings. Add tomato sauce, corn, wine, salt, pepper, and chili powder. Simmer gently for 20 minutes, stirring occasionally.

2. Pour mixture into six individual casseroles. Combine cornbread mix with amount of water recommended on package. Add ½ cup of the grated cheese. Top casserole with cornbread mixture.

3. Bake in a 400 degree oven 20 minutes. Remove from oven and sprinkle with remaining cheese and corn chips. Bake 10 minutes longer.

Makes six servings.

CARRY-ALONG CRUSTLESS QUICHE

8 eggs
1 cup light cream
Salt and pepper, to taste
10 slices bacon
½ pound mushrooms, thinly sliced, or 2
    cans (4 ounces each) mushrooms
1 package (8 ounces) American cheese
    slices
Paprika

1. Beat eggs. Add cream, salt, and pepper and beat thoroughly.

2. Cook bacon until lightly browned and crisp. Drain on paper towels.

3. Crumble bacon. Add to egg mixture with mushrooms.

4. Butter a 9 x 13-inch baking dish. Line bottom and sides with slices of American cheese. Pour egg mixture over cheese slices. Sprinkle with paprika.

5. Bake in a 350 degree oven 30 minutes or until lightly browned and puffy. Serve warm or cold.

Makes four to six servings.

CINCINNATI QUICHE

1 9-inch unbaked pie shell
3 eggs
½ cup milk
½ cup light cream
¾ teaspoon salt
½ teaspoon Tabasco
⅛ teaspoon nutmeg
¼ pound Swiss cheese, grated
¼ pound Gruyere cheese, grated
1 tablespoon flour
1 large onion, cut into quarters and
    thinly sliced

1. Preheat oven to 450 degrees.

2. Prick pie shell all over with a fork. Bake 5 to 10 minutes or just until delicately brown. Remove pie shell. Reduce oven heat to 325 degrees.

3. Beat eggs, milk, cream, salt, Tabasco, and nutmeg together. Combine grated cheese and flour. Spread evenly in pie shell. Pour on cream mixture. Top with onion slices.

4. Bake 45 minutes or until point of a knife inserted in pie comes out clean.

STADIUM SLOPPY JOES

1½ pounds lean ground beef
1½ teaspoons salt
½ teaspoon curry powder
1 medium tomato, finely chopped
1 small cucumber, grated
1 small onion, finely chopped
⅓ cup catsup
⅓ cup sweet pickle relish
8 hamburger buns, toasted

1. Lightly brown ground beef in a skillet on a hibachi or small grill at moderate temperature. Pour off any excess drippings.

2. Add salt, curry powder, tomato, cucumber, onion, catsup, and relish. Mix well. Cover and cook 15 minutes, stirring occasionally.

3. Serve on toasted buns.
Makes eight servings.

GIANTS BEEF-PEPPER SANDWICHES

2 cans (11 ounces each) condensed
    onion soup
½ cup water
2 medium green peppers, cut in strips
½ teaspoon basil leaves
¼ teaspoon pepper
2 pounds thinly sliced cooked roast beef
8 to 12 Italian style or French hard rolls,
    split

1. Combine onion soup, water, green pepper, basil, and pepper in a frying pan and simmer on top of a hibachi or small grill for 15 minutes.

2. Add meat and heat.

3. To serve, dip cut surfaces of rolls in hot cooking liquid. Place slices of hot beef and green pepper strips between roll halves and serve at once.

Makes 8 to 12 servings.

STEELERS SUBMARINES

4 pounds lean ground beef
2 small onions, chopped
2 packages (1½ to 1¾ ounces each) taco seasoning mix
2 teaspoons salt
1 can (15 ounces) tomato sauce
2 cups sharp Cheddar cheese, grated
1 cup stuffed green olives, sliced
2 loaves unsliced French or Italian bread

1. Lightly brown ground beef and onions in a frying pan or Dutch oven. Pour off any drippings.

2. Sprinkle taco seasoning and salt over meat. Add tomato sauce, 1 cup shredded cheese, and olives. Cook 5 to 10 minutes, stirring occasionally.

3. Slice loaves of bread in half lengthwise. Remove soft bread to form boats, hollowing inside of loaves until sides and bottom are about three-quarters of an inch thick. Make 2 cups of crumbs from removed bread and stir into meat mixture.

4. Spoon meat mixture into bread boats. Round the top. Sprinkle remaining cup of cheese over meat. Wrap each boat loosely in heavy-duty aluminum foil.

5. At a tailgate party, place on grill or hibachi and heat 20 to 25 minutes or until piping hot.

6. Remove submarines from foil and cut into slices about one and a quarter inches thick.

Makes 16 to 20 servings of two slices each.

LEMON MIST CHEESE PIE

3 eggs, separated
1½ cups creamed cottage cheese
⅔ cup light cream
3 tablespoons lemon juice
1 teaspoon lemon rind, grated
⅔ cup sugar
1 tablespoon flour
¼ teaspoon salt
1 unbaked 9-inch pie shell

1. Put egg yolks in a large bowl and whites in a small bowl. Beat egg whites

with mixer until whites are stiff but not dry. Set aside.

2. With same beaters, beat yolks until well blended. Add cottage cheese, cream, lemon juice, and lemon rind. Beat until thoroughly mixed. Add sugar, flour, and salt, and beat until well mixed.

3. Fold in egg whites with a rubber scraper. Pour mixture into unbaked pie shell.

4. Bake in a 450 degree oven for 10 minutes. Reduce heat to 325 degrees and bake 35 to 40 minutes or until a knife inserted in center of pie comes out clean.

Makes six to eight servings.

CHOCOLATE CHIP CAKE

1 package (18½ ounces) chocolate, double chocolate, or fudge cake mix
1 box (3½ ounces) instant chocolate pudding mix
½ cup sour cream
4 eggs
½ cup salad oil
½ cup warm water
1 package (6 ounces) semi-sweet chocolate morsels

1. Lightly oil a 10-inch bundt or tube pan. Set aside. Preheat oven to 350 degrees.

2. Place cake mix, pudding mix, sour cream, eggs, salad oil, and warm water in large electric mixer bowl. Mix at low speed until ingredients are well blended. Beat at medium speed three minutes. Turn batter into prepared pan.

3. Bake 45 to 55 minutes or until a toothpick inserted in cake comes out clean.

4. Let cake stand five minutes. Turn out of pan onto a cooling rack. Cake can be eaten warm or cool.

BRING-FROM-HOME BROWNIES

1 cup butter or margarine
4 squares unsweetened chocolate
2 cups sugar
4 eggs
2 teaspoons vanilla
1½ cups all-purpose flour
1 cup nuts, chopped (optional)
¼ cup confectioners' sugar

1. Melt butter and chocolate in a large saucepan over low heat.

2. Remove from heat and stir in sugar. Cool slightly.

3. Add eggs, one at a time, beating thoroughly after each addition.

4. Add vanilla and blend well.

5. Slowly stir in flour and nuts. Mix until smooth.

6. Butter a 9 x 13-inch baking pan. Spread brownie mixture evenly in pan. Bake in a 350 degree oven 30 minutes. Do not overbake.

7. Cool slightly. Sprinkle with confectioners' sugar and cut into squares.

Makes 30 brownies.

CHARGERS COCONUT TARTS

1⅓ cups all-purpose flour
1 cup sugar
¼ teaspoon salt
¾ cup butter
1 egg, slightly beaten
1 egg
1 can (3½ ounces) flaked coconut

1. Sift flour with ⅓ cup sugar and salt in mixing bowl. With a pastry blender, cut in butter until mixture resembles coarse crumbs. With a fork, stir in beaten egg. Knead slightly until mixture holds together. Wrap in waxed paper. Refrigerate several hours or until firm.

2. With a fork, beat egg in a small bowl. Add coconut and remaining ⅔ cup sugar. Mix well.

3. For each tart, pinch off about 1 teaspoon chilled dough. Press into a 2 x ½-inch tart pan to make a shell one-eighth-inch thick. Fill each shell with 1 teaspoon filling. Set tarts on a baking sheet.

4. Bake in 375 degree oven for 12

minutes or until coconut filling is lightly browned.

5. Place pans on wire rack; cool slightly. With small spatula, gently remove tarts from pans.

Makes four dozen tarts.

DOLPHINS LEMON BARS

2¼ cups all-purpose flour, divided
½ cup confectioners' sugar
1 cup firm butter or margarine
2 cups sugar
½ teaspoon baking powder
4 eggs, beaten
6 tablespoons lemon juice

1. Preheat oven to 350 degrees.
2. Mix together 2 cups of the flour with confectioners' sugar in a bowl. Cut in butter with a pastry blender or two knives. When mixture looks like cornmeal, turn into an ungreased 9 x 12 x 3-inch baking pan. Press mixture down firmly on bottom of pan.
3. Bake 20 minutes.
4. Mix together the remaining ¼ cup flour with the sugar and baking powder. Add to beaten eggs and mix well. Beat in lemon juice.
5. Pour over baked crust. Bake 25 minutes. Cool about 30 minutes. Cut into squares. Dust with confectioners' sugar before serving.

Makes about 24 squares.

PINEAPPLE DROP COOKIES

1 cup brown sugar, firmly packed
½ cup mixed shortening and butter
1 egg
1 teaspoon vanilla
¾ cup crushed canned pineapple
2 cups all-purpose flour
1 teaspoon baking powder
½ teaspoon baking soda
½ teaspoon salt
¾ cup chopped walnuts
½ cup seedless raisins

1. Stir together sugar, shortening, egg, and vanilla until blended. Add pineapple, with as little syrup as possible, and stir well.

2. Sift together flour, baking powder, baking soda, and salt. Stir into sugar mixture. Add walnuts and raisins.

3. Drop by the heaping teaspoonful on an ungreased baking sheet. Bake in a 375 degree oven for 12 minutes or until lightly browned.

4. Makes three dozen cookies.

BROWNS OLD-TIME COOKIES

1 cup butter or margarine
2 cups brown sugar, firmly packed
4 eggs
4 cups all-purpose flour
1 teaspoon baking soda
1½ teaspoons nutmeg
½ teaspoon salt
¼ cup milk
2 cups seedless raisins
1 cup chopped nuts

1. Cream together butter and brown sugar until fluffy. Beat in eggs.

2. Sift flour, soda, nutmeg, and salt together. Add to creamed mixture alternately with milk, beating well after each addition. Stir in raisins and nuts.

3. Drop by the teaspoonful onto a lightly greased baking sheet.

4. Bake in a 375 degree oven 10 to 12 minutes or until lightly browned.

5. Remove from baking sheet and cool on racks.

Makes about five dozen cookies.

BANANA-OATMEAL DROPKICK COOKIES

¾ cup shortening
1 cup sugar
1 egg
1 medium-sized banana, mashed
½ teaspoon lemon juice
1½ cups all-purpose flour
½ teaspoon baking soda
½ teaspoon salt
¾ teaspoon cinnamon
¼ teaspoon nutmeg
1½ cups quick-cooking oats
½ cup chopped walnuts

1. Cream together shortening and sugar until fluffy. Beat in egg. Stir in banana and lemon juice.

2. Sift together flour, soda, salt, cinnamon, and nutmeg. Stir into creamed mixture. Mix in oats and walnuts.

3. Drop by the teaspoonful onto a greased baking sheet, two inches apart.

4. Bake in a 350 degree oven 12 to 15 minutes or until edges turn golden brown.

Makes about four dozen cookies.

BIG APPLE GINGER BARS

1 package gingerbread mix
1 can (8½ ounces) applesauce
½ cup raisins
1 jar (4 ounces) mixed candied fruits and peels
2 cups sifted confectioners' sugar
Milk
1 teaspoon lemon juice
1 teaspoon lemon peel, grated

1. Preheat oven to 375 degrees.

2. Combine gingerbread mix and applesauce and beat until well blended. Stir in raisins and candied fruits.

3. Spread in a greased 15½ x 10 x 1-inch pan. Bake 15 to 20 minutes.

4. Combine confectioners' sugar with enough milk to make it of spreading consistency. Stir in lemon juice and peel. Spread thinly over baked gingerbread. Cut into bars.

Makes 40 bars.

BARBECUES
WHEN ARMCHAIR QUARTERBACKS BECOME BACKYARD GOURMETS

By the time NFL players are returning to training camps in July, most barbecue chefs are hitting their strides. After weeks of outdoor cooking practice, the steaks and hamburgers are coming off the grill done to perfection, the ribs and chicken no longer resemble the coals in the fire, and experiments have begun with marinades and skewers.

Though NFL training camps and the smell of backyard barbecues smoking away are sure-fire signs of summer, outdoor barbecue cooking is by no means exclusively summertime fare. Hardy football fans in cold northern climes have braved blizzards to grill hot dogs and, in the South, many a barbecue meal has been prepared during monsoon rains under the shelter of a carport.

One thing all successful barbecue chefs—and NFL players—have in common is timing. The barbecue fire, in particular, must be timed right; it should be started about 20 to 30 minutes before cooking is to begin. For halftime cooking, that means getting the fire going at the beginning of the second quarter. This is also a good time to serve cheeses, dips, or hors d'oeuvres.

For a good barbecue fire, line the grill base with heavy duty aluminum foil, then pile briquets in a pyramid in the center. Light the coals according to the instructions on the charcoal bag. The fire is ready when the coals are covered with fine ash and glowing in the center. Before cooking, spread out the coals so heat will be even.

A number of other factors can affect food prepared on an outdoor grill and should be taken into consideration. Cooking time will vary with the cut and type of meat, weather, heat of the coals, position on the grill, and height of the grill from the coals.

NEW ENGLAND CLAM DIP

2 packages (3 ounces each) cream
  cheese
1 teaspoon salt
½ teaspoon Tabasco sauce
1 tablespoon onion, grated
1 can (7½ ounces) minced clams
1 cup dairy sour cream

    1. Place cream cheese in a small
bowl and let soften at room temperature.
    2. Blend in salt, Tabasco, and onion.
Drain clams, reserving 2 teaspoons of
the clam liquor. Add clams and the
reserved liquor to cream cheese. Stir in
sour cream and blend well.
    3. Turn into a serving dish and chill
30 minutes before serving.
    4. Serve with crisp sticks of celery,
cucumber, white turnip, carrots, small
whole scallions, and/or zucchini slices.
    Makes two cups dip.

SEATTLE SMOKEY SALMON SPREAD

1 can (7¾ ounces) salmon
1 package (8 ounces) cream cheese,
  softened
1 tablespoon lemon juice
2 teaspoons onion, grated
2 teaspoons horseradish, grated
¼ teaspoon liquid smoke
Salt and pepper to taste
¼ cup pecans, chopped
2 tablespoons parsley, snipped

    1. Drain and flake salmon. Add
cream cheese, lemon juice, onion,
horseradish, liquid smoke, and salt and
pepper to taste. Blend thoroughly.
    2. Shape mixture into a ball on
waxed paper. Wrap and chill for several
hours.
    3. Combine pecans and parsley on
a square of waxed paper. Roll salmon
ball in mixture to coat on all sides.
    4. Place on a serving plate with
assorted crackers.
    Makes one-half cup.

CHEESY FOOTBALL

3 pounds cream cheese
¼ cup toasted almonds, finely chopped
¼ cup walnuts, finely chopped
2 to 3 tablespoons Grand Marnier

1. Place cream cheese in a bowl and let soften at room temperature.

2. Add remaining ingredients and mix thoroughly.

3. Mold mixture into a football shape. Place on a serving platter and surround with greens. Refrigerate long enough to make cheese firm.

4. Serve with crispy crackers.

BARBECUED BEEF SANDWICHES

3 to 3½ pounds lean round steak
1 bottle (12 ounces) barbecue sauce
3 onions, thinly sliced
Sourdough or sandwich-size hard rolls

1. Put meat in a 9 x 13-inch baking pan. Cover with barbecue sauce and onions. Refrigerate six hours, turning occasionally.

2. Put steak on barbecue grill over hot coals. Cook six minutes. Turn steak and cook six more minutes or to desired degree of doneness.

3. Remove steak to carving board. Slice thinly in crosswise strips. Serve on hard rolls with any leftover sauce.

Makes 10 to 12 sandwiches.

LINEBACKER STEAK

6 tenderloin steaks, about ½–1 pound
    each, fat removed
¼ cup Worcestershire sauce
6 wide thin strips salt pork, long enough
    to go around steaks

1. Brush each steak with Worcestershire sauce. Wrap a thin strip of salt pork around each steak. Tie with string or fasten with toothpicks.

2. Grill over hot coals, about four inches from source of heat, until desired degree of doneness is almost reached.

3. Remove steaks from grill. Discard pork. Return steaks to grill to brown.

Makes six servings.

LEMON 'n' SPICE BEEF STEAKS

⅔ cup lemon juice
½ cup water
1 tablespoon oil
1 tablespoon sugar
1½ teaspoons salt
1 teaspoon thyme
¼ teaspoon garlic powder
1 or 2 beef blade steaks, cut ½-
   to ¾-inch thick

1. Combine lemon juice, water, oil, sugar, salt, thyme, and garlic powder in a small saucepan. Cook slowly for five minutes. Cool.

2. Place steaks on a flat baking pan or in a plastic bag. Pour marinade over steaks, turning to coat. Cover dish or tie bag securely and marinate in refrigerator six hours or overnight, turning at least once.

3. Remove steaks from marinade. Place on grill so surface of meat is four inches from heat. Broil at moderate heat 7 to 10 minutes on each side, depending on desired degree of doneness. Brush steaks with remaining marinade occasionally during broiling time.

Makes three to six servings.

KANSAS CITY TERIYAKI STICKS

4- to 5-pound chuck roast, 1½ inches
   thick, frozen
1 cup soy sauce
½ cup liquid brown sugar
5 thin slices fresh ginger root, peeled
Garlic salt
Vinegar
Green onions
50 12-inch teriyaki sticks or long wooden
   skewers

1. Partially defrost meat until it is sliceable but still firm. Slice meat as thin as possible. Cut away all fat and gristle. Cut slices of meat into 1-inch lengths.

2. Put soy sauce and sugar into a saucepan. Add ginger, a pinch of garlic salt, and about 1 teaspoon vinegar. Taste and add more sugar or vinegar as needed.

3. Bring mixture to a boil. Remove

from heat and cool.

4. Place meat in a large bowl. Pour cooled sauce over meat. Slice tops only of a few green onions into ¼-inch lengths and add to meat. Stir.

5. Refrigerate overnight. Stir occasionally.

6. Thread a teriyaki stick through each piece of meat at least twice. Put three or four pieces of meat on a stick, covering about eight inches of the stick. Leave four inches at end of stick to hang over barbecue grill.

7. Place sticks over hot charcoal and cook to taste, turning once. Serve.

Makes 50 sticks.

CLEVELAND BEEF AND CHEESE DOGS
2 pounds lean ground beef
1 cup Monterey Jack cheese, shredded
1½ teaspoons salt
⅛ teaspoon pepper
1 small onion, chopped
½ cup Russian dressing
¼ cup horseradish mustard
6 hot dog buns, toasted, if desired

1. Combine ground beef, cheese, salt, and pepper. Divide into six equal portions and mold into rolls the shape of frankfurters.

2. Place on grill and broil at moderate temperature 20 to 25 minutes or to desired degree of doneness, turning occasionally.

3. Combine onion, Russian dressing, and mustard in a small saucepan. Cook on grill 10 minutes, stirring occasionally.

4. Serve beef rolls on hot dog buns accompanied with sauce.

Makes six servings.

STUFFED SUPERBURGERS

1 package (3 ounces) cream cheese
¼ cup dairy sour cream
½ teaspoon dill weed
2 cups toasted bread cubes
¼ cup mushrooms, chopped
¼ cup pitted ripe olives, chopped
1 tablespoon instant minced onion
⅓ cup water
2 teaspoons salt
¼ teaspoon pepper
2 pounds lean ground beef

1. Mix together cream cheese, sour cream, and dill weed. Stir in toasted bread cubes, mushrooms, and olives. Stir instant minced onion into water and let stand five minutes. Sprinkle salt and pepper over ground beef, add onion and water and combine lightly.

2. Shape meat mixture into 12 thin patties five to six inches in diameter. Place an equal amount of cheese stuffing in center of each of six patties. Top with remaining patties, pressing edges together to seal.

3. Place burgers on grill three to four inches from heat and broil 8 to 12 minutes on each side or to desired degree of doneness.

Makes six servings.

76

RAMS BARBECUED RIBS

4½ to 5 pounds spare ribs
Salt
Pepper
Rosemary
½ cup honey
¼ cup lemon juice
¼ cup Worcestershire sauce
¼ cup sherry

1. Cut ribs into sections of 4 or 5 ribs each. Sprinkle with salt and pepper. Rub with rosemary.

2. Combine honey, lemon juice, Worcestershire sauce, and sherry.

3. Place ribs, meat side up, on grill over low heat. Brush with sauce mixture and turn frequently. Cook slowly until ribs are crisp, brown, and thoroughly cooked, (about one to one and a half hours).

Makes four servings.

BENGALS BARBECUED SHORT RIBS

1 tablespoon dry mustard
¼ teaspoon garlic powder
½ teaspoon chili powder
¼ teaspoon cayenne pepper
3½ cups catsup
¼ cup lemon juice
4 pounds beef short ribs
½ cup molasses

1. Combine mustard, garlic powder, chili powder, pepper, catsup, and lemon juice in a large bowl. Add short ribs and toss well. Refrigerate several hours.

2. Lift ribs from marinade and place on metal skewers. Leave a space of about one inch between each rib.

3. Place ribs on grill over medium hot coals and broil slowly, turning often to cook evenly.

4. Add molasses to remaining marinade and brush onto short ribs about 10 minutes before cooking is finished. It will take about 40 minutes to cook the ribs.

5. Serve remaining sauce with ribs.

Makes four servings.

PACKERS GRILL-TOP GARDEN POT ROAST

1 package (0.6 ounces) Italian salad
   dressing mix
¼ cup flour
1½ teaspoons salt
½ teaspoon paprika
Freshly ground pepper to taste
3- to 4-pound beef blade roast
2 cups carrots, thinly sliced
2 cups zucchini, sliced ¾-inch thick

1. Combine salad dressing mix, flour, 1 teaspoon salt, paprika, and pepper. Thoroughly dredge meat on both sides. Place meat in center of a double thick rectangle of heavy-duty aluminum foil (twice the circumference and eight inches longer than the roast). Sprinkle any remaining flour mixture over meat. Bring two opposite edges of foil together over top of meat. Fold edges over three to four times, pressing crease in tightly each time; allow some air space. Flatten foil at one end, crease to form triangle and fold edge over several times toward package, pressing tightly to seal.

Repeat procedure at other end.

2. Place on grill and cook at low to moderate temperature one and one half hours, turning after one hour.

3. Remove foil packet from grill. Open carefully and add carrots and zucchini. Sprinkle ½ teaspoon salt on vegetables. Close foil, sealing securely. Place on grill, vegetable side up, and continue cooking 30 minutes or until meat and vegetables are done.

Makes four to six servings.

LIONS BUTTERFLIED LAMB

1 5-pound boned leg of lamb
2 cloves garlic
1 teaspoon sugar
2 cups dry white wine
½ cup vinegar
1 teaspoon pepper
1 teaspoon salt
2 tablespoons olive oil
½ bunch fresh mint, chopped

1. Have butcher bone and flatten lamb to about one and one-half-inch thickness.

2. Cut garlic in very thin slices. Cut gashes in lamb with point of sharp knife and insert garlic in cuts. Combine remaining ingredients in a deep bowl. Add lamb, turning to coat well. Cover and refrigerate several hours or overnight, turning lamb several times.

3. Remove lamb from marinade and place on grill, cut-side down, five to six inches from hot coals. Grill 20 minutes, basting several times with marinade. Turn and grill 20 more minutes, basting with marinade.

4. To serve, cut in slices crosswise. Makes 8 to 10 servings.

Variation: Do not marinate lamb. Brush with a little oil and sprinkle with rosemary and broil according to directions.

SKEWERED LAMB CUBES

3- to 3½-pound leg of lamb
1 cup dry red wine
Salt
Freshly ground black pepper
1 tablespoon dried tarragon
2 tablespoons red wine vinegar
2 tablespoons olive oil
1 garlic clove, minced
12 to 16 mushroom caps
Melted butter
Fresh lemon juice

1. Bone leg of lamb. Remove fat and skin. Cut meat into 1-inch cubes. Put cubes in a large bowl.

2. Add wine, salt and pepper to taste, tarragon, vinegar, oil, and garlic. Let stand several hours.

3. Arrange a mushroom cap on each of six or eight skewers. Arrange equal portions of lamb cubes on each of the skewers. Add a mushroom cap at end of skewer.

4. Cook over hot coals for about 10 minutes, turning often, or to desired degree of doneness.

5. Brush with melted butter and a squeeze of lemon juice and serve at once.

Makes six to eight servings.

CHALLENGE PORK CHOPS

2 tablespoons salt
2 tablespoons sugar
2 tablespoons monosodium glutamate
1 tablespoon freshly ground black
   pepper
2 tablespoons dry lemon powder
1 tablespoon paprika
6 pork chops, 1-inch thick
3 tablespoons white wine

1. Combine salt, sugar, monosodium glutamate, pepper, lemon powder, and paprika. Sprinkle chops well on both sides with this mixture.

2. Place chops on grill over hot coals. Grill until brown and seared on both sides, turning frequently.

3. Pour wine into a heavy skillet. Add pork chops. Place pan on grill over hot coals. If using a covered barbecue, cover; if not, cover the frying pan with aluminum foil. Cook about 30 minutes or until chops are very tender.

Makes six servings.

Note: After browning chops, each one can be placed on a square of aluminum foil. Add a small amount of white wine and seal packets. Place directly on grill and cook about 30 minutes.

ITALIAN SAUSAGE WITH GREEN PEPPERS AND ONIONS

1½ to 2 pounds sweet and/or hot Italian
   sausage
½ cup butter or margarine
2 green peppers, sliced into strips
1 large onion, sliced
9 to 12 Italian rolls

1. Cook sausages on a barbecue grill, three to four inches from hot charcoal, turning frequently to cook evenly.

2. While sausage is cooking, melt butter in a heavy skillet on grill. Add green pepper and onion and cook just until onion is tender.

3. Slice rolls in half lengthwise and toast lightly on grill. Place a sausage on each roll and top with green peppers and onions.

Makes 9 to 12 servings.

CARNE ASADA BURRITO

2 2-pound ribeye or New York cut steaks
Salt and pepper
Garlic powder
2 roasted tomatoes, peeled and
    chopped
1 roasted onion, peeled and chopped
1 roasted green bell pepper, peeled
    and chopped
1 small red hot pepper, seeded and
    chopped very fine
3 sprigs fresh cilantro
½ teaspoon ground cilantro
1 teaspoon salt
Pinch granulated garlic
Pinch ground cloves
Pinch ground white pepper
Corn or flour tortillas, heated

1. Cut steaks in thin slices, about ¼-inch thick. Sprinkle with salt, pepper, and garlic powder. Refrigerate about one hour.

2. Combine tomatoes, onion, green pepper, red hot pepper, cilantro, dried cilantro, salt, garlic, cloves, and white pepper. Let stand.

3. Broil meat on an outdoor grill, about five to six inches from hot charcoal. Cook to desired degree of doneness.

4. Place two tablespoons of tomato mixture just below center of each tortilla. Top with desired amount of meat, depending on size of tortilla and number of people to be served.

5. Fold sides of tortilla over filling. Fold up bottom flap, then roll tightly as for a jelly roll. Serve with chilled guacamole, if desired.

Makes six to eight servings.

TAMPA BAY SUNSHINE PORK KABOBS

1 cup bottled barbecue sauce
1 cup orange juice
⅓ cup lemon juice
⅓ cup brown sugar
2 tablespoons soy sauce
2 tablespoons instant minced onion
1 teaspoon salt
2- to 2½-pound boneless pork shoulder,
    cut into 1¼-inch pieces
18 to 24 small canned onions
1 large orange, cut in six wedges

1. To prepare marinade, combine barbecue sauce, orange juice, lemon juice, brown sugar, soy sauce, onion, and salt. Stir.

2. Place meat in a plastic bag or bowl. Pour marinade over meat, turning to coat. Tie bag securely or cover bowl and marinate in refrigerator one to three hours.

3. Drain marinade from meat into a small saucepan. Bring to a boil, lower heat and simmer, uncovered, 10 to 20 minutes, stirring occasionally until sauce thickens.

4. Alternately thread pieces of pork and onions on six 12-inch metal skewers. Place on grill five to seven inches from hot coals. Broil at moderate heat 25 to 30 minutes, turning and brushing with sauce occasionally. Place an orange wedge on end of each skewer, brush with sauce, and continue cooking about five minutes or until meat is done, turning once.

Makes six servings.

OILERS CHICKEN BREASTS

½ cup butter
2 tablespoons vinegar
1 teaspoon Worcestershire sauce
1 teaspoon seasoned salt
¼ teaspoon paprika
½ teaspoon garlic powder
Dash Tabasco sauce
Freshly ground black pepper
8 half chicken breasts

1. Melt butter in a small saucepan. Add vinegar, Worcestershire sauce, seasoned salt, paprika, garlic powder,

Tabasco sauce, and a grind of pepper. Blend.

2. Place chicken breasts skin-side down on barbecue grill over hot coals. Baste and turn frequently until chicken is cooked, 25 to 30 minutes, depending on heat of coals and distance from coals.

Makes four to six servings.

SUPER STUFFED PORK CHOPS

6 to 8 pork rib chops, cut
   1¼ to 1½-inches thick
1 package (7 ounces) cornbread
   stuffing mix
⅓ cup honey
1 tablespoon prepared mustard
1 tablespoon lemon juice
Salt and pepper

1. Make a pocket in each chop by cutting into the chop on rib side parallel to the surface of the chop. Be careful not to cut through the opposite side.

2. Prepare stuffing according to package directions, using amount of water specified for less moist stuffing. Cool.

3. To prepare glaze, combine honey, mustard, and lemon juice in a small saucepan and cook five minutes to thicken.

4. Stuff pocket in each chop with an equal amount of the stuffing mixture.

5. Place chops on grill about five to seven inches from hot coals and cook at low to moderate temperature 20 minutes, turning occasionally.

6. Season chops on both sides with salt and pepper. Broil 10 to 15 minutes longer, or until chops are done, brushing with honey glaze and turning occasionally.

Makes six to eight servings.

CHIEFS CHICKEN

1 cup soy sauce
¼ cup brown sugar
2 tablespoons honey
2 tablespoons sugar
4 slices ginger root, peeled
1 clove garlic, minced
1 teaspoon vinegar
2 broiler-fryer chickens, cut in serving
  pieces

1. Combine soy sauce, brown sugar, honey, sugar, ginger root, garlic, and vinegar in a saucepan. Bring to a boil. Remove from heat and cool.

2. Put chicken pieces in a large bowl. Add cooled sauce mixture. Refrigerate several hours or overnight. Stir occasionally.

3. Put chicken pieces on a grill over hot charcoal, skin-side down. Cook about 20 minutes. Turn chicken and continue cooking about 25 minutes or until chicken is browned and cooked. Brush occasionally with remaining marinade, if desired.

Makes about eight servings.

POLLO ADOVADO

½ cup dry vermouth
2½ teaspoons ground cinnamon
⅓ cup honey
2 tablespoons lime juice
1 clove garlic, crushed
1 teaspoon salt
1 broiler-fryer chicken, cut in serving
  pieces

1. Combine vermouth, cinnamon, honey, lime juice, garlic, and salt in a mixing bowl.

2. Add chicken pieces and toss to cover each piece of chicken. Cover and refrigerate four to six hours. Turn chicken pieces occasionally.

3. Cook chicken on a grill, four to six inches from hot charcoal. Cook about 40 minutes, turning frequently during cooking time. Brush chicken with marinade several times during cooking time.

Makes four servings.

LOS ANGELES BARBECUED SHRIMP

Large shrimp or prawns
Lemon juice
Celery salt
Black pepper
Melted butter

1. Split, but do not remove, shrimp shells. Place shrimp in a bowl. Add lemon juice, celery salt, pepper, and let stand six to eight hours, tossing occasionally.

2. Cook on a grill about four to six inches from hot coals until shrimp turn bright red.

3. Serve piping hot with melted butter.

SEAHAWKS SALMON STEAKS

⅓ cup butter, melted
3 tablespoons lemon juice
1 tablespoon parsley, finely snipped
1 teaspoon dill weed
¼ teaspoon salt
Grind of fresh pepper
6 salmon steaks, about ¾-inch thick

1. Combine butter, lemon juice, parsley, dill weed, salt, and pepper. Place salmon steaks in a flat baking pan. Pour mixture over top. Turn salmon. Marinate one hour at room temperature or several hours in the refrigerator. Turn occasionally.

2. Remove salmon from marinade. Place on grill about four to six inches from hot coals. Cook 8 to 14 minutes, turning once and basting often with marinade, until fish flakes easily when tested with a fork.

3. Serve with lemon wedges.
Makes six servings.

GRILLED CHICKEN BREASTS WITH DIJON SAUCE

3 whole chicken breasts, split in half
¼ cup butter or margarine, melted
2 tablespoons lemon juice
¼ teaspoon thyme leaves
1 teaspoon instant minced onion
½ teaspoon salt
¼ teaspoon pepper
⅓ cup dairy sour cream
⅓ cup mayonnaise
2 tablespoons dill pickle, finely chopped
1 tablespoon Dijon mustard
2 tablespoons green onion, finely
   chopped

1. Tear off six lengths of heavy-duty aluminum foil large enough to wrap a chicken breast. Place one chicken breast half, skin-side up, on each square of foil.

2. Combine butter, lemon juice, thyme, onion, salt, and pepper. Brush each piece of chicken with mixture. Turn chicken over and brush other side. Leave chicken skin-side down on foil.

3. Bring four corners of foil up together in a pyramid shape. Fold the openings together loosely to allow for heat circulation and expansion. Seal by folding over ends and pressing to package.

4. Place on grill over medium hot coals and cook 30 to 45 minutes or until chicken is tender.

5. While chicken is cooking combine sour cream, mayonnaise, pickle, and mustard.

6. To serve, remove chicken from foil bundles and spoon sauce over top.

7. Sprinkle with green onions and serve at once.

Makes six servings.

GRANDSTAND POTATOES

4 medium potatoes
3 tablespoons butter or margarine
½ cup heavy cream
Salt and pepper
Parsley, chopped
½ cup Cheddar cheese, grated

1. Peel potatoes and cut into thin strips as for French fries. Place in center of a large piece of heavy-duty aluminum foil. Dot with butter, add cream, seasonings, parsley, and cheese.

2. Bring two sides of foil up over potatoes. Fold down loosely in a series of locked folds, allowing for heat circulation. Fold short ends up and over again; crimp to seal.

3. Place on grill over hot coals. Grill 30 to 40 minutes, turning two or three times, or until potatoes are tender. Open package carefully, fold back and shape into a dish to serve potatoes.

Makes four servings.

GRILLED SQUASH PARMESAN

3 small yellow squash, washed and
    sliced ¼-inch thick
10 cherry tomatoes, halved
½ teaspoon oregano
2 tablespoons grated Parmesan cheese
¼ teaspoon salt
Grind of fresh pepper
2 tablespoons butter or margarine

1. Combine all ingredients except butter in center of an 18-inch square of heavy-duty aluminum foil. Dot with butter.

2. Bring four corners of foil up together in pyramid shape. Fold the openings loosely to allow for heat circulation. Seal by folding over ends and pressing to the package.

3. Place on grill over medium hot coals and grill 20 to 30 minutes or until squash is tender.

Makes six servings.

REDSKINS ROASTED HERB CORN

6 ears fresh corn
¼ cup butter or margarine, melted
1 teaspoon dried crumbled parsley
¼ teaspoon crumbled rosemary leaves
½ teaspoon sugar
½ teaspoon paprika
½ teaspoon salt

1. Remove husks from corn. Place each ear in a square of heavy-duty aluminum foil.

2. Combine remaining ingredients. Spread over ears of corn. Wrap each ear tightly.

3. Place on grill four to six inches from hot coals. Roast, turning very often, 15 to 25 minutes or until cooked.

Makes six servings.

ROLLOUT VEGETABLE PACKETS

2 medium tomatoes, sliced ½-inch thick
2 medium zucchini, cut in ¼-inch slices
2 medium onions, thinly sliced
2 medium green peppers, cut in rings
12 mushrooms, halved
Salt and pepper
Basil
4 teaspoons butter or margarine

1. Alternately place slices of tomato, zucchini, onion, and green pepper in an overlapping row on each of four 9 x 12-inch pieces of heavy-duty aluminum foil. Top each with mushrooms. Season with salt, pepper, and basil and top each with 1 teaspoon butter. Close foil packets with a double fold. Turn up ends and fold to close securely.

2. Place on grill and cook at moderate temperature 15 to 20 minutes or until vegetables are done.

Makes four servings.

ASPARAGUS VINAIGRETTE

6 tablespoons salad oil
3 tablespoons white wine vinegar
⅛ teaspoon Tabasco sauce
½ teaspoon sugar
¼ teaspoon salt
1 small onion, thinly sliced and broken
    into rings
2 dozen cooked asparagus spears

1. Combine salad oil, vinegar, Tabasco, sugar, and salt and mix until well blended. Add onion rings.

2. Arrange asparagus spears in a shallow serving dish. Pour dressing over asparagus. Let stand in refrigerator several hours, or overnight.

Makes six servings.

ONION-APPLE AUDIBLES

Onions, medium sized, peeled
Apples, unpared, cut into wedges
Brown sugar
Lemon juice
Butter or margarine
Salt

1. For each serving, slice one onion halfway down into quarters. Insert an unpared tart apple wedge between each quarter.

2. Place each onion on a square of heavy-duty aluminum foil. Top each with 1 tablespoon brown sugar, ½ teaspoon lemon juice, 1 teaspoon butter or margarine, and a pinch of salt. Wrap securely and place onions on a grill over hot coals and cook 45 minutes to one hour or until onions are tender.

COWBOYS BEAN SALAD

1 can (20 ounces) chick peas, drained
2 cans (1 pound each) cut green beans, drained
1 large sweet red onion, thinly sliced
¾ cup salad oil
⅓ cup vinegar
1 teaspoon salt
¼ teaspoon dry mustard
½ teaspoon paprika
⅛ teaspoon freshly ground pepper

1. Combine chick peas, green beans, and onion in a large bowl.
2. Combine remaining ingredients and beat well to blend flavors. Add to vegetables and toss lightly.
3. Refrigerate two to three hours before servings.
Makes 10 servings.

GREEK SALAD

1½ quarts torn salad greens, washed and drained
2 cucumbers, peeled and sliced
6 green onions, chopped
Salt and pepper to taste
Olive oil
Lemon juice
8 small radishes, cleaned and sliced
3 tomatoes, quartered
16 anchovy fillets
16 pitted Greek olives
½ pound feta cheese, crumbled

1. Place salad greens in a large bowl and mix in cucumbers and green onions. Season with salt and pepper. Dress with combined oil and lemon juice in proportions to suit your taste, using just enough to coat greens nicely.
2. Arrange remaining ingredients on top. Just before serving, toss lightly.
Makes eight servings.

SOUTHERN SLAW

1 large head cabbage
1½ cups cooked ham, chopped
1 green pepper, seeded and chopped
1 sweet red pepper, seeded
 and chopped
1 large onion, chopped
Salt and pepper to taste
1 egg white
1 cup mayonnaise, or to taste

1. Chop cabbage finely. Add ham, green pepper, red pepper, and onion. Season with salt and pepper. Refrigerate until just before time to serve.

2. Beat egg white until frothy. Use to thin mayonnaise. Add to cabbage mixture and toss well.

Makes eight servings.

MANDARIN ORANGE SALAD

½ head lettuce, shredded
1 cup celery, chopped
1 tablespoon parsley, minced
2 green onions, including tops, sliced
1 can (11 ounces) mandarin oranges,
 drained
½ teaspoon salt
Grind of fresh pepper
¼ teaspoon hot pepper sauce
2 tablespoons tarragon vinegar
¼ cup salad oil
¼ cup toasted almonds, chopped

1. Place lettuce, celery, parsley, onions, and mandarin oranges in a salad bowl.

2. Combine remaining ingredients in a jar with a tight fitting cover. Shake well. Pour over ingredients in salad bowl and toss lightly.

Makes four servings.

HASHMARKS BEAN SALAD

2 cans (20 ounces each) cannolini
   beans (Italian white beans)
2 large red onions, chopped
1½ cups celery, chopped
¾ cup stuffed olives, sliced
Salt and pepper to taste
½ cup olive oil
3 tablespoons white wine vinegar
Parsley, snipped

   1. Drain beans. Mix with onions,
celery, and olives. Season well.
   2. Combine oil and vinegar. Pour
just enough over salad to coat the
ingredients well. Refrigerate overnight.
   3. Remove from refrigerator one
hour before serving. Sprinkle with
parsley.
   Makes eight servings.

49ERS POTATO SALAD

4 large potatoes, peeled and cut into
   ½-inch cubes
1 cup mayonnaise
1 teaspoon prepared mustard
3 tablespoons dill pickle juice
1 tablespoon sweet pickle relish
1 cucumber, peeled and diced
1 large ripe tomato, peeled
   and chopped
4 large radishes, thinly sliced
4 green onions, sliced
1 medium dill pickle, chopped
3 hard-boiled eggs, sliced
Paprika

   1. Cook potato cubes in boiling
salted water just until tender. Do not
overcook. Drain.
   2. Combine mayonnaise, mustard,
dill pickle juice, and pickle relish. Add
to still warm potatoes and toss lightly. Let
stand at room temperature 20 minutes.
Refrigerate for two hours.
   3. Add remaining ingredients,
except one of the eggs and paprika.
Toss lightly. Garnish with egg slices and
paprika.
   Makes four to six servings.

DETROIT PUMPKIN PIE

1 package (8 ounces) cream
  cheese, softened
¾ cup brown sugar, firmly packed
1 teaspoon cinnamon
1 teaspoon nutmeg
½ teaspoon ginger
½ teaspoon salt
3 eggs
1 cup canned pumpkin
1 cup milk
1 unbaked nine-inch pie shell
Heavy cream, whipped

1. Place cheese, brown sugar, spices, and salt in bowl of an electric mixer. Blend until smooth and then beat for one minute.

2. Add eggs, one at a time, beating well after each addition. Add pumpkin and milk and blend well.

3. Pour mixture into unbaked pie shell. Bake in a 375 degree oven 45 to 50 minutes or until a knife inserted in center of pie comes out clean.

4. Serve chilled with whipped cream, if desired.

PEACH TARTS

2 eggs, well beaten
2 cups dairy sour cream
½ teaspoon vanilla
¼ teaspoon almond extract
1 cup peach preserves
12 unbaked three-inch pastry shells
Toasted slivered almonds
Whipped cream (optional)

1. Combine eggs, sour cream, vanilla, and almond extract. Blend well. Fold in preserves. Spoon mixture into pastry shells. Sprinkle with almonds.

2. Bake in a 350 degree oven 25 to 30 minutes or until mixture is set.

3. Refrigerate before serving. Serve with whipped cream, flavored with almond extract.

Makes 12 servings.

CHOCOLATE RUM MOUSSE

1 cup milk, divided
1 envelope unflavored gelatin
6 tablespoons dark rum
1 egg
¼ cup sugar
⅛ teaspoon salt
1 package (6 ounces) semisweet
  chocolate pieces
1 cup heavy cream
2 ice cubes

1. Put ¼ cup of milk in a blender. Add gelatin and let stand until gelatin is softened.

2. Heat the remaining ¾ cup milk to boiling. Add hot milk gradually to softened gelatin, beating until gelatin is dissolved. If gelatin granules cling to sides of container, stop blender and use a rubber spatula to push them down into liquid.

3. Add rum, egg, sugar, salt, and chocolate pieces. Process until mixture is smooth. Add cream and ice cubes and process until ice is liquefied.

4. Pour into a one and one-half-quart dessert dish. Chill until firm. Serve with flavored whipped cream, if desired. Makes eight servings.

CHERRY STARR'S COCONUT BUTTERMILK CAKE*

½ cup butter or margarine
½ cup shortening
2 cups sugar, divided
5 eggs, separated
1 teaspoon vanilla
2 cups all-purpose flour
1 teaspoon baking soda
½ teaspoon salt
1 cup buttermilk
1 can (3½ ounces) flaked coconut
1 cup chopped pecans

1. Lightly grease three nine-inch cake pans. Line with circles of waxed paper and grease again. Preheat oven to 375 degrees.

2. Cream butter and shortening together in a large mixing bowl. Add 1½ cups sugar gradually and beat until light and fluffy. Add egg yolks and

vanilla and beat thoroughly.

3. Sift together flour, baking soda, and salt. Add to creamed mixture alternately with buttermilk, beating mixture smooth after each addition.

4. Beat egg whites until stiff but not dry. Beat in remaining ½ cup sugar. Fold egg whites gently into batter. Fold in coconut and pecans.

5. Turn batter into greased cake pans. Bake 25 minutes or until done when tested with a toothpick. Remove from oven and let stand about 10 minutes. Turn out of cake pans to finish cooling.

6. Fill and frost cake with desired icing.

*Cherry Starr is the wife of Green Bay Packers head coach Bart Starr.

MIAMI MACAROON PEACHES

1 can (16 ounces) peach halves, drained
⅔ cup macaroon cookies, crushed
2 tablespoons butter or margarine, softened
¼ teaspoon ground nutmeg
¼ teaspoon ground cinnamon

1. For each serving, place 2 peach halves in center of a length of heavy-duty aluminum foil large enough to permit adequate wrapping. Combine remaining ingredients; sprinkle ⅓ of the mixture over peaches. Bring four corners of foil up together in a pyramid shape. Fold the openings together loosely to allow for heat circulation and expansion. Seal by folding over ends and pressing to package. Repeat process.

2. Place on grill over medium hot coals and grill 15 to 20 minutes or until peaches are hot.

Makes about three servings.

BILLS COTTAGE PUDDING

¼ cup butter or margarine, softened
½ cup sugar
1 egg
1⅔ cups all-purpose flour
2 teaspoons baking powder
½ teaspoon salt
½ cup milk
Chocolate sauce or raspberry preserves

1. Preheat oven to 350 degrees. Grease an eight-inch square baking pan.

2. Cream together butter and sugar until light and fluffy. Beat in egg. Stir together flour, baking powder, and salt. Add to egg mixture alternately with milk, beating well after each addition. Pour mixture into prepared pan.

3. Bake 20 to 25 minutes or until a tester inserted in center comes out clean.

4. Cut warm pudding into nine squares and serve with chocolate sauce or preserves.

Makes nine servings.

SWEDISH APPLE CAKE

1 cup butter or margarine
⅓ cup sugar
1¾ cups all-purpose flour
½ cup Zwieback crumbs
½ teaspoon salt
2 cups applesauce
¾ cup light brown sugar, firmly packed
1 teaspoon cinnamon
1 teaspoon grated lemon peel
2 eggs, separated
¼ teaspoon salt
1 cup raspberry preserves
½ cup slivered, blanched almonds

1. Combine butter, sugar, flour, crumbs, and ½ teaspoon salt to make a crumbly dough. Measure ⅔ cup of this mixture and spread in a small pan. Press remaining mixture firmly in a lightly buttered 12 x 8 x 2-inch pan. Bake in a 375 degree oven for 20 minutes or until golden brown.

2. At the same time bake the small pan of crumbs 10 to 12 minutes or until lightly browned.

3. Combine applesauce, ½ cup of

the brown sugar, cinnamon, lemon peel, and the egg yolks in a saucepan. Cook over low heat, stirring constantly, until thickened, about 12 to 15 minutes.

4. Beat egg whites until stiff. Gradually beat in the remaining ¼ cup brown sugar and the ¼ teaspoon salt. Beat until egg whites are very stiff.

5. Spread applesauce mixture over baked crust. Sprinkle with toasted crumbs. Spoon on raspberry preserves. Spread meringue carefully over top. Sprinkle with almonds.

6. Bake in a 400 degree oven four to six minutes or until meringue is lightly browned. Cool and cut into squares.

TEXAS BROWNIES
1 cup butter or margarine
2 squares unsweetened chocolate
4 eggs
2 cups sugar
Pinch salt
2 tablespoons vanilla
1 cup all-purpose flour
1 cup nuts, chopped

Icing:
¼ cup cocoa
¼ cup butter or margarine
1 cup sugar
¼ cup milk
1 teaspoon vanilla

1. Grease and lightly flour a 13 x 9 x 3-inch baking pan. Place a pan of hot water on lowest shelf of oven. Preheat oven to 350 degrees.

2. Place butter and chocolate in top part of double boiler. Cook over hot water until chocolate is melted. Cool.

3. Beat eggs in a mixing bowl. Beat in sugar, salt, and vanilla. Add cooled chocolate. Fold in flour and nuts and blend thoroughly.

4. Pour mixture in prepared pan. Place on rack in center of oven. Bake 45 minutes or until a toothpick inserted in center comes out clean. Remove from oven.

5. Combine icing ingredients, except vanilla. Bring to a boil and cook one minute. Add vanilla and beat a few minutes to cool. Pour over brownies. Cool and cut into squares.

MONDAY NIGHT DINNERS
PRIME MEALS FOR
PRIME TIME FOOTBALL

From September through December, Monday night is pro football night. More and more people are taking advantage of the game's prime-time kickoff by hosting all kinds of get-togethers centered around good food and NFL action. When Monday night football began in 1970 (the Cleveland Browns beat the New York Jets 31-21 in the first telecast), few suspected that it would become as much a social as a sports event. But, after all, it is the only game in town.

Depending on where you live, the game's starting time may determine the type of Monday night entertaining you do. For example, in the West the games are telecast early enough to allow for serving cocktails, hors d'oeuvres, and a halftime formal, sit-down dinner. In the Midwest, a serve-yourself buffet may fit the kickoff time better. And in the East, with the games' later starts, a dessert and coffee party would be a good alternative to continental-hours dining.

As for most NFL-related entertaining, the Monday night dinner menu can be as unpretentious or as elegant as you wish. A nice idea is to give the meal a distinctly regional or international flavor with such recipes as chili (have a chili taste-off between three or four different recipes), Zakuski and Chicken Kiev, Beef Stroganoff, New Orleans or Houston-style red beans and rice or Turkey Andouille gumbo, Lomo de Puerco, or Chicken Cacciatore.

Or, around the holiday season, try a traditional American menu featuring such favorites as pork chops or Cornish hens with raisin stuffing, sweet potatoes flambé or squash soufflé, and baked Alaska or pecan pie.

Just ask those Monday night veterans of more than a decade ago: it all beats take-out pizza!

WASHINGTON WON TONS

½ pound ground pork
¼ cup soy sauce
6 green onions, minced
4 small stalks celery, minced
1 can (4½ ounces) tiny shrimp, drained
    and finely chopped
1 package won ton skins
4 cups oil for frying
Hot mustard sauce
Sweet and Sour sauce

1. Fry pork over medium heat until cooked, stirring. Drain off fat. Add soy sauce, onions, celery, and shrimp. Heat, stirring. Remove from heat and cool.

2. Remove one won ton skin at a time from package. Keep remaining skins covered with a damp cloth. Dampen one side of skin with water. Place about 1 teaspoon filling in center of dampened side of skin. Fold and bring up two sides of won ton skin and pinch firmly all around. Pull the two bottom edges together and pinch firmly to seal, using a little water to hold. Repeat process with remaining skins. Cover finished won tons with a damp cloth.

3. Heat oil in a wok or a deep fat fryer, to 350 degrees. Cook a few won tons at a time until crisp and lightly browned (about five minutes). When browned and cooked, remove and drain on paper towels. Keep hot in a 200 degree oven.

4. Serve with mustard sauce or Sweet and Sour sauce.

Makes 40 to 50 won tons.

MINNESOTA MUSHROOMS

1 large onion, minced
1 clove garlic, minced
2 cups dry white wine
½ cup cider vinegar
2 bay leaves
½ teaspoon thyme
½ teaspoon pepper
½ teaspoon salt
½ cup olive oil
1½ pounds button mushrooms

1. Combine onion, garlic, wine, vinegar, bay leaves, thyme, pepper, and

salt in a small saucepan. Bring to a boil and simmer five minutes. Add oil.

2. Wash mushrooms and pat dry. Remove stems and reserve for another use. Put caps in wine-vinegar mixture. Simmer until mushrooms are barely tender (8 to 10 minues).

3. Refrigerate until ready to serve. Makes four servings.

ZAKUSKI (Poor Man's Caviar)
1 medium eggplant
Water
½ cup onion, chopped
½ cup salad oil
½ teaspoon salt
Pepper to taste
¼ cup tomato sauce

1. Cook whole eggplant for 15 minutes in a saucepan with enough water to cover. When tender, drain. Peel off skin and chop very fine.

2. Fry onion in hot oil until golden brown. Add eggplant, salt, pepper, and tomato sauce. Mix well and simmer

over low heat about 10 minutes. Chill.

3. To serve, place chilled eggplant mixture in a small dish. Serve with small squares of Russian rye bread or rye crackers.

Makes six servings.

KICKOFF CHICKEN WINGS

3 pounds chicken wings
½ cup salad oil
½ cup lemon juice
1 clove garlic, crushed
1 teaspoon salt
⅛ teaspoon pepper
½ cup stuffed olives, chopped

1. Cut chicken wings apart at both joints; reserve tips for soup stock.

2. Combine disjointed wing pieces with remaining ingredients in a large bowl. Marinate several hours or overnight in the refrigerator, turning occasionally.

3. Arrange wing pieces on a rack in a shallow roasting pan. Roast in a 450 degree oven 35 to 40 minutes or until crisp and brown. Spoon marinade over wings several times during roasting period.

Makes about 28 pieces.

WILTED GREENS SALAD

Iceberg lettuce, butter lettuce, and/or fresh spinach leaves
2 tablespoons bacon drippings, butter, or margarine
2 eggs, lightly beaten
1 cup light cream or half-and-half
¼ cup white wine vinegar
1 teaspoon sugar (optional)
Salt and pepper to taste
4 slices cooked bacon, crumbled

1. Wash lettuce and spinach thoroughly. Drain leaves and either spin dry or pat dry. Tear into bite-size pieces and put in a salad bowl. There should be about six cups of greens.

2. Combine bacon drippings, eggs, cream, vinegar, sugar, salt, and pepper in a small saucepan. Heat over low heat, stirring constantly, until mixture is thickened. Do not allow mixture to boil.

3. Pour hot dressing over greens and toss lightly. Sprinkle bacon over top and serve immediately.

Makes four to six servings.

SILVERDOME CAESAR SALAD

½ pound bacon, cut up
¼ cup olive oil
1 tablespoon fresh lemon juice
¼ teaspoon salt (optional)
½ teaspoon freshly ground black
   pepper
¼ teaspoon Worcestershire sauce
⅛ teaspoon dry mustard
1 clove garlic, cut in half
1 large bunch Romaine lettuce, washed
   and crisped
½ pound fresh spinach, rinsed
   and crisped
1 egg, at room temperature
⅓ cup grated Parmesan cheese
1 cup packaged seasoned croutons
6 anchovy fillets, cut in half (optional)
1 medium tomato, cut into wedges

1. Cook bacon in a large skillet until lightly browned and crisp. Drain on paper towels.

2. Combine olive oil, lemon juice, salt, pepper, Worcestershire sauce, and mustard. Blend well. Set aside.

3. Rub a salad bowl with cut side of garlic. Tear Romaine and spinach into bite-size pieces. Place in a bowl, cover, and refrigerate.

4. Bring about three inches of water to a rolling boil in a small saucepan. Remove from heat and add egg. Cover pan and let stand three minutes. Cover with cold water and let stand.

5. Add the coddled egg to the olive oil mixture and whip until well blended. Pour dressing over greens and toss until leaves are well coated with dressing.

6. Add bacon bits, cheese, croutons, and anchovies. Toss lightly. Garnish with wedges of tomato. Serve salad at once.

Makes six servings.

COLTS CRANBERRY-ORANGE DELIGHT

1 package (6 ounces) raspberry- or strawberry-flavored gelatin
2 cups hot cranberry juice cocktail
2 cups bitter lemon carbonated beverage
1 cup walnuts, chopped
1 cup raw cranberries, chopped
1 can (11 ounces) mandarin oranges, well drained

1. Dissolve gelatin in hot cranberry juice. Stir in bitter lemon beverage and refrigerate until partially set.
2. Fold in remaining ingredients. Pour into a one and one-half-quart mold. Chill until firm. Unmold on lettuce.
Makes 8 to 10 servings.

OILERS RED BEANS, RICE, AND SAUSAGE

1 pound red kidney beans
2 quarts water
3 large ham hocks
½ pound lean pork, cut in small pieces
½ cup green onions, finely chopped
2 large onions, chopped
1 rib celery, chopped
1 large bay leaf
2 tablespoons parsley, chopped
4 cloves garlic, minced
2 teaspoons salt
½ teaspoon freshly ground black pepper
½ teaspoon dried crushed red pepper
1½ pounds hot Italian sausage, cut into three-inch lengths
Hot cooked rice

1. Rinse and pick over beans. Place in a heavy kettle or Dutch oven. Add water, ham hocks, and pork. Bring to a boil. Reduce heat and simmer about 25 minutes.
2. Add onions, celery, bay leaf, parsley, garlic, salt, and black and red pepper. Simmer about two hours or until beans are tender. Stir occasionally during cooking time, adding more water if necessary.
3. Simmer sausage in a skillet in a small amount of water about 20 minutes, or until thoroughly cooked.
4. Serve beans and sausage over hot cooked rice.

REDMOND RED CHILI

2 pounds lean ground chuck
1 large onion, chopped
1 large green pepper, chopped
1 can (1 pound) tomatoes
1 can (16 ounces) tomato sauce
1 can (6 ounces) tomato paste
1 cup water
5 tablespoons cumin
6 tablespoons chili powder
Salt and pepper to taste
Hot jalapeño peppers, diced (optional)
2 cans (16 ounces each) pinto beans
1 pound small button mushrooms,
   cleaned

1. Brown meat, onion, and green pepper in a Dutch oven over high heat, stirring occasionally. Drain off any accumulated fat.

2. Add tomatoes, tomato sauce, tomato paste, water, cumin, chili powder, salt, pepper, and jalapeños, if desired.

3. Bring mixture to a boil, stirring occasionally. Lower heat and simmer 15 minutes.

4. Add beans and mushrooms. Bring to a boil. Lower heat and simmer 10 minutes.

   Makes eight servings.

Note: Those who prefer hotter chili may add chili powder and jalapeños to taste. But it is best to begin mild and work up to hot, particularly if you are serving guests with unfamiliar tastes.

STAN WEST'S CHILI

1 package (2 pounds) kidney beans
2 pounds lean ground beef
2 cans (8 ounces each) tomato sauce
3 tomato sauce cans water
1 package (1¾ ounces) chili spices,
   blended

1. Soak beans overnight and cook according to package directions.

2. Brown meat in a large skillet, stirring occasionally. Pour off any excess fat.

3. Add tomato sauce, water, and spices according to package directions. Simmer mixture 1½ hours.

3. When cooked to desired consistency, serve alone or over hot cooked beans.

GRIDIRON CHILI

½ pound dried pinto beans
2 cans (16 ounces each) tomatoes, chopped
1 pound green peppers, coarsely chopped
1½ pounds onions, coarsely chopped
1½ tablespoons oil
2 cloves garlic, crushed
½ cup butter or margarine
2½ pounds lean ground chuck
1 pound lean ground pork
⅓ cup chili powder
2 tablespoons salt
1½ teaspoons pepper
1½ teaspoons ground cumin
½ cup parsley, finely chopped

1. Wash and pick over beans. Cover with water and let stand overnight.

2. Place beans and water in a saucepan. Bring to a boil, lower heat, and simmer just until tender. Add tomatoes and simmer five minutes.

3. In a skillet, cook green peppers and onions in hot oil just until tender, stirring frequently. Add garlic and cook three minutes.

4. In another skillet, melt the butter. Add chuck and pork and cook, stirring frequently, about 10 minutes. Add meat to onion mixture, stir in chili powder, and cook 10 minutes.

5. Add meat mixture to cooked beans. Add salt, pepper, cumin, and parsley. Cover and simmer 30 minutes. Remove cover and skim any excess fat from top of chili. Heat 10 minutes more.

Makes 10 servings.

BO BOLINGER'S RED HOT CORNBREAD

1½ cups yellow cornmeal
1 teaspoon baking powder
1 teaspoon salt
1 teaspoon sugar
½ teaspoon baking soda
1 can (8 ounces) cream style corn
¾ cup milk
⅓ cup vegetable shortening, melted
2 eggs, slightly beaten
1½ cups Cheddar cheese, grated
1 can (4 ounces) green chiles,

chopped, or 1 can (6 ounces) jalapeño peppers, chopped

1. Lightly grease and flour an 8 x 11-inch baking pan. Preheat oven to 375 degrees.
2. Combine cornmeal, baking powder, salt, sugar, and baking soda in a mixing bowl.
3. In another bowl mix corn, milk, shortening, and eggs. Pour into dry mixture and blend well. Stir in cheese and chiles or peppers.
4. Pour mixture into baking pan. Bake 30 minutes or until a toothpick inserted in center comes out clean.

Makes four to six servings.

NEW ORLEANS RED BEANS AND RICE
2 pounds red beans
½ pound lean country ham, diced
3 smoked ham hocks
2 large onions, chopped
½ teaspoon Tabasco sauce
1 bay leaf
2 ribs celery, finely chopped
Pinch thyme
Salt to taste
Freshly ground black pepper
Hot cooked rice

1. Soak beans in water to cover overnight.
2. Drain beans. Cover beans again with water, then add 2 more cups water. Bring beans to a boil. Add ham, ham hocks, onions, Tabasco sauce, bay leaf, celery, and thyme. Return to a boil. Reduce heat and simmer three to four hours, stirring occasionally.
3. Remove 1 to 2 cups beans and mash well. Add a small amount of liquid from kettle and stir into beans to make a smooth paste. Return to soup pot and stir. Season with salt to taste.
4. Heat thoroughly. Serve over hot cooked rice, with sausage if desired.

Makes eight servings.

ERBY AUCOIN'S TURKEY ANDOUILLE GUMBO

1 cup salad oil
1 cup flour
3 large onions, finely chopped
1 large green pepper, chopped
2 stalks celery, chopped
4 quarts water
4 to 5 pounds cooked turkey
3 pounds Andouille sausage, kielbasa, or any smoked sausage, cut in ¼-inch-thick slices
½ cup parsley, finely chopped
2 cups green onions, chopped and divided
2 cloves garlic, finely chopped
Tabasco sauce to taste
1 pint oysters (optional)
½ pound package frozen okra (optional)
Filé (ground sassafras leaves)
Hot cooked rice

1. Heat oil in a large Dutch oven. Add flour slowly and stir well. Cook slowly over medium heat, stirring, until mixture turns a dark brown color. Add onions and cook until onions are soft.

2. Add green pepper, celery, water, turkey, Andouille (pronounced ON-dewey) sausage or substitute, parsley, 1 cup of the green onions, garlic, Tabasco, oysters, and okra, if desired.

3. Cook about one and one-half hours, stirring occasionally.

4. To serve, put cooked rice in individual serving dishes. Sprinkle with about ½ teaspoon filé and green onions. Top with a healthy serving of gumbo.

Makes 12 to 14 servings.

Note: The ingredient that makes this dish so special is Andouille ham, a lean, highly smoked meat that is similar to Canadian bacon. It is difficult to obtain outside of the New Orleans area, but the substitutes suggested in the recipe come very close to giving the dish its authentic flavor.

According to Erby Aucoin, the New Orleans Saints' cinematographer, the real secret to his gumbo is the way the roux (flour paste) is made. "The secret is to get it as brown and rich as a rich chocolate paste," he says. "Get the oil hot, then add the flour slowly, stirring constantly, and have a great deal of patience. Also be careful with the seasonings. Start light and go on from there. You can add, but you can't take it out."

BUFFALO STUFFED CABBAGE
2 medium onions, chopped
2 tablespoons salad oil
3 cans (8 ounces each) tomato sauce
3 cups water
1 can (16 ounces) tomatoes
Pepper and salt to taste
½ cup brown sugar, firmly packed
1½ cups raisins
¼ cup lemon juice
1 large head cabbage
2½ pounds lean chopped beef
⅔ cup raw rice
½ cup gingersnap crumbs

1. Cook onions in 2 tablespoons salad oil in a Dutch oven or large heavy kettle, just until soft but not browned. Add tomato sauce, water, tomatoes, pepper and salt, brown sugar, raisins, and lemon juice. Bring to a boil. Lower heat and simmer 30 minutes.

2. Remove core from cabbage and carefully remove leaves. Immerse cabbage leaves in boiling water about three minutes, or until limp. Drain. Cut out center vein, keeping each leaf in one piece. Set aside.

3. Combine beef and rice. Season with a little salt and pepper. Add about 1 cup of the tomato gravy and blend well. Place 1 tablespoon of the meat mixture in center of each cabbage leaf. Roll up and fasten with a clove. Place cabbage rolls carefully in pot holding gravy.

4. Simmer over moderate heat, covered, about one and one-half hours, or until cooked.

5. Remove cabbage leaves to a warm serving dish. Stir gingersnap crumbs into gravy in pan. Bring to a boil, stirring. Served with stuffed cabbage.
Makes 12 to 14 servings.

SZECHUAN SHRIMP

½ cup green onions, minced
½ cup bamboo shoots, minced
3 cloves garlic, minced
¼ teaspoon fresh ginger, minced
½ teaspoon liquid hot pepper sauce
2 tablespoons sugar
½ cup catsup
3 tablespoons dry sherry
1 tablespoon soy sauce
1½ teaspoons sesame oil
1 tablespoon cornstarch
3 tablespoons water
1½ cups peanut oil
1 pound fresh shrimp, shelled and
  deveined

1. Combine onions, bamboo shoots, garlic, ginger, and hot pepper sauce in a small bowl. Mix well.

2. Combine sugar, catsup, sherry, soy sauce, and sesame oil in a bowl.

3. Combine cornstarch and water in a bowl. Stir well.

4. Heat peanut oil in a large skillet or wok to 400 degrees. Have a bowl and strainer ready for use.

5. Add shrimp to hot oil and cook, stirring constantly, until done (about two minutes). Turn into strainer over bowl and drain well.

6. Heat 2 tablespoons of the oil over high heat. Add scallion-bamboo mixture; stir-fry one minute. Add strained shrimp and stir-fry 30 seconds. Add catsup mixture and cook 30 seconds.

7. Stir up cornstarch and water. Add to shrimp mixture and cook, stirring constantly, until thickened.

8. Serve over hot cooked rice. Makes four servings.

SHARON ALZADO'S CRAB-SHRIMP BAKE*

1 onion, chopped
1 green pepper, chopped
1 cup celery, chopped
1 can (7 ounces) crab meat, drained
  and picked over
1 can (4½ ounces) shrimp, drained
1 cup mayonnaise
1 teaspoon Worcestershire sauce
½ teaspoon salt

Dash of paprika
⅛ teaspoon pepper
1 cup dry bread crumbs
2 teaspoons butter, melted
1 cup Cheddar cheese, grated
   (optional)

1. Combine onion, pepper, celery, crab meat, shrimp, mayonnaise, Worcestershire sauce, salt, paprika, and pepper. Pour mixture into a one-quart lightly buttered casserole.

2. Toss bread crumbs with melted butter. Sprinkle over top of casserole. Add Cheddar cheese, if desired.

3. Bake in a 350 degree oven 30 minutes or until hot and bubbly.

Makes four to six servings.

*Sharon Alzado is the wife of Cleveland defensive end Lyle Alzado.

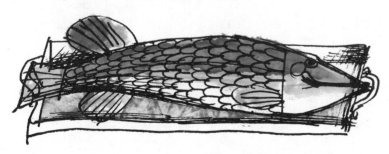

PAT GRANT'S PARMESAN PIKE*

3 pounds walleyed pike filets or any
   white fish filets
1 cup dairy sour cream
¼ cup butter or margarine, melted
½ cup Parmesan cheese, grated
½ teaspoon salt
½ teaspoon pepper
Parsley, chopped

1. Wipe pike filets with a damp cloth. Pat dry. Place in a lightly buttered baking pan.

2. Combine sour cream, butter, cheese, salt, and pepper. Spread over filets in baking pan.

3. Bake in a 350 degree oven 30 minutes. Remove from oven and sprinkle with parsley. Serve immediately.

Note: Try substituting low-fat buttermilk or low-fat plain or lemon-flavored yogurt in place of the sour cream.

*Pat Grant is the wife of Minnesota Vikings head coach Bud Grant.

SENEGALESE CHICKEN

1 broiler-fryer chicken, cut in serving
   pieces
Juice of 5 lemons or limes
1/3 cup cider vinegar
2 tablespoons black peppercorns
1/4 cup salad oil
5 onions, thinly sliced
Crushed red pepper, to taste

1. Place chicken in a shallow baking pan. Add lemon juice, vinegar, and peppercorns. Toss well. Cover and refrigerate 24 hours, tossing occasionally to coat the chicken pieces with marinade.

2. Remove chicken pieces. Heat oil in a large skillet or Dutch oven. Brown chicken pieces on all sides in hot oil. Remove chicken. Cook onions in hot oil until soft and lightly browned.

3. Return chicken to Dutch oven with any remaining marinade. Cover and simmer about one hour, or until chicken is tender.

4. Add red pepper to taste. Serve with hot cooked rice.

CHICKEN KIEV A LA DENISE

6 chicken breasts, boned and skinned
2 tablespoons parsley, finely chopped
1½ teaspoons tarragon
1 clove garlic, minced
¾ teaspoon salt
⅛ teaspoon freshly ground pepper
1 cup butter
Flour
3 to 4 eggs, beaten
1½ cups bread crumbs
Cooking oil

1. Cut chicken breasts in half lengthwise. Put chicken breasts between two pieces of waxed paper. Pound with the side of cleaver or a heavy kettle to ¼-inch thickness.

2. Combine parsley, tarragon, garlic, salt, pepper, and butter and blend well. Shape into a flat block and freeze. When firm, cut into 12 cubes and freeze until hard.

3. Place each chicken piece on a flat surface, outside down. Place a cube of butter on chicken and roll chicken to encase butter. Fold in ends. Secure with

toothpicks or tie with string. Roll each chicken breast in flour, dip in beaten eggs, and then roll in bread crumbs. Refrigerate chicken for at least one to two hours.

4. Put about three inches of oil in a large skillet. Heat to 325°. Deep-fry two to three chicken breasts at a time for five to seven minutes, or until golden brown.

5. Drain on paper towels and keep warm in a warm oven for serving.

Makes six servings.

PLAYOFF CORNISH HENS
4 Rock Cornish hens
Salt and pepper
Raisin Stuffing
Melted butter or margarine

1. Preheat oven to 350 degrees.
2. Remove giblets. Season with salt and pepper inside and out.
3. Stuff with Raisin Stuffing. Truss birds. Place breast side up on a rack in a shallow roasting pan. Brush with melt-ed butter. Roast 75 minutes, or until birds are tender. Baste occasionally during cooking time. Raise oven temperature to 400 degrees during last 10 minutes of cooking time to brown birds.

Makes four servings.

RAISIN STUFFING
1 cup white or golden raisins
½ cup cognac
¾ cup butter or margarine
½ cup shallots, chopped
1 teaspoon salt
3 cups cooked rice
½ cup pistachio nuts, shelled
   and chopped

1. Soak raisins in cognac 10 minutes. Drain, reserving cognac. Melt butter in a skillet. Add raisins and shallots and sauté a few minutes.

2. Add remaining ingredients, including cognac. Toss lightly to mix.

Makes enough stuffing for four Cornish hens. Put any leftover stuffing in a baking dish. Heat and serve as a side dish.

SEA BASS SAN DIEGO

4 sea bass filets
Salt
Pepper
Flour
1 egg, beaten
½ pound mushrooms, sliced
1 clove garlic, minced
¼ cup butter or margarine
½ cup dry white wine
1 teaspoon lemon juice
Olive oil

1. Sprinkle filets with salt and pepper. Dust filets on both sides with flour. Dip in beaten egg and recoat with flour. Set aside.

2. Sauté mushrooms and garlic in butter just until tender. Add white wine and lemon juice and simmer gently.

3. Heat olive oil in a large skillet. Fry filets gently for about six to eight minutes on each side or until fish flakes easily when tested with a fork.

4. Serve filets topped with mushroom mixture.

Makes four servings.

CHICKEN CACCIATORE CHICAGO

½ cup flour
½ teaspoon salt
Grind of fresh pepper
3½ pound broiler-fryer chicken, cut in
   serving pieces
¼ cup olive or salad oil
1 large onion, sliced
1 clove garlic, crushed
1 can (1 pound) peeled tomatoes,
   mashed
1 cup mushrooms, sliced
½ cup dry white or red wine
1 tablespoon Italian parsley, chopped
¼ teaspoon dried oregano or rosemary
Hot cooked rice

1. Combine flour, salt, and pepper. Coat chicken pieces with this mixture.

2. Heat oil in a large, heavy skillet. Brown chicken on all sides. Remove chicken.

3. Sauté onion and garlic in hot oil just until tender but not browned. Return chicken to skillet. Add tomatoes. Cover skillet and simmer 45 minutes.

4. Add mushrooms, wine, parsley,

and oregano. Season to taste with salt and pepper. Continue cooking for 10 minutes or until chicken is tender and sauce is blended. Serve with hot cooked rice.

Makes four servings.

LOMO DE PUERCO
2 pound loin of pork
2 slices cooked ham, cut into thin strips
2 slices bacon, cooked lightly and cut in strips
2 pickled jalapeño peppers, chopped
8 whole cloves
Salt and pepper
2 small onions, minced
1 clove garlic, crushed
3 tablespoons red chili powder
1 tablespoon sugar
Few drops lime juice
½ cup beef broth

1. Make several incisions in fat side of pork loin. Stuff each incision with strips of ham, bacon, and chopped jalapeños. Place a whole clove in some incisions.

2. Sprinkle with salt and pepper.

3. Combine onion, garlic, chili powder, sugar, and lime juice to make a paste. Rub paste on meat.

4. Place meat on a rack, fat-side up, in a shallow roasting pan. Roast at 350 degrees, allowing 30 to 35 minutes per pound, or until a meat thermometer reads 180 degrees.

5. Remove meat to a serving platter and keep warm.

6. Skim off excess fat from liquid in roasting pan. Add broth and simmer gently for a few minutes. Serve with roast pork.

Makes six servings.

HOUSTON PORK CHOPS AND SPANISH RICE

5 pork chops, about ½-inch thick
1 tablespoon shortening
1 teaspoon salt
½ teaspoon chili powder
Grind of fresh pepper
¾ cup uncooked long-grain rice
½ cup onion, chopped
¼ cup green pepper, chopped
1 can (28 ounces) tomatoes, chopped
5 green pepper rings
½ cup American, Longhorn, or Colby cheese, grated

1. Trim excess fat from chops. Heat shortening in a large, heavy skillet. Add chops and brown slowly about 10 minutes on each side. Drain off excess fat.

2. Sprinkle salt and chili powder over chops. Add pepper, rice, onion, chopped green pepper, and tomatoes.

3. Cover and cook over low heat about 35 minutes, stirring occasionally, or until rice is tender.

4. Add green pepper rings and cook five minutes longer.

5. Sprinkle with cheese just before serving.

Makes five servings.

VEAL DIJONNAISE

¾ to 1 pound veal scallopine
Vegetable oil
½ pound mushrooms, cleaned and thinly sliced
2 teaspoons Dijon mustard
Pinch garlic salt
Pinch ground black pepper
¼ cup light cream
Pinch sage

1. Place veal between two squares of waxed paper. Pound very thin with the side of a cleaver or a heavy kettle.

2. Heat a small amount of oil in a skillet until hot. Lightly brown veal on both sides. Remove from pan and keep warm on a warm platter.

3. Sauté mushrooms in oil in same skillet just until cooked. Add remaining ingredients and bring to a boil. Pour over veal and serve at once.

PERNICANO'S PORK CHOPS

Center cut pork chops, trimmed of all
   fat, cut 1-inch thick
Salt
Pepper
Garlic clove, cut

1. Sprinkle pork chops with salt and pepper. Rub cut side of garlic clove on both sides of pork chops.

2. Broil chops four to five inches from source of heat 10 minutes for each side.

3. Place chops on a baking pan. Bake in a 500 degree oven five minutes.

FAIR CATCH STEW

2 pounds calf round steak or scallops cut
   from beef eye round
½ cup flour
Salt and pepper
2 tablespoons sweet paprika
4 tablespoons olive oil
1 can (4 ounces) sliced mushrooms
1 beef bouillon cube
1 can (8 ounces) tomato sauce
¼ cup green pepper, chopped
1 package (8 ounces) egg noodles
Parmesan cheese, grated

1. Put beef between two sheets of waxed paper. Pound with the side of a cleaver or a heavy pot.

2. Combine flour, salt, pepper, and sweet paprika. Dust meat on both sides with this mixture.

3. Heat 3 tablespoons of olive oil in a heavy skillet and brown the meat on both sides. As browned, remove to a large flat baking dish.

4. Drain mushrooms, saving liquid. Add enough water to liquid to make 1 cup. Bring liquid to a boil. Add bouillon cube and stir. Pour over beef. Bake in a 350 degree oven 30 minutes.

5. Combine mushrooms, tomato sauce, and green pepper. Pour over the meat and cook for 15 minutes.

6. Cook noodles in boiling salted water with the remaining olive oil.

7. Drain noodles. Turn out on a heated serving platter. Place meat on top of noodles and pour sauce over meat and noodles. Sprinkle with Parmesan cheese.

GREEN BAY BEEF STROGANOFF

1 tablespoon dry mustard
2 teaspoons sugar
Salt
Water
Salad oil
4 cups onion, thinly sliced and
   separated into rings
1 pound mushrooms, thinly sliced
2 pound filet of beef
½ teaspoon freshly ground black
   pepper
2 cups dairy sour cream

   1. In a small bowl combine dry mustard, 1½ teaspoons of the sugar, and a pinch of salt. Stir in about 1 tablespoon water to make a thick paste. Set aside.

   2. Heat 2 tablespoons oil in a heavy 12-inch skillet over high heat until oil is smoking. Add onions and mushrooms. Reduce heat, cover pan, and simmer 25 minutes, stirring occasionally. Drain mixture in a sieve, return to a skillet, and set aside.

   3. Cut filet across the grain into slices about ¼-inch thick. Cut each slice into ¼-inch wide strips.

   4. Heat 2 tablespoons oil in another heavy 12-inch skillet over high heat until it is hot, but not smoking. Drop in half the meat strips and fry two minutes, tossing constantly until meat is lightly browned. Transfer meat to skillet holding vegetables. Fry remaining meat, adding more oil if necessary.

   5. When meat and vegetables are combined, stir in ½ tablespoon salt, ½ teaspoon pepper, and the mustard mixture.

   6. Stir in sour cream, a small amount at a time. Add remaining ½ teaspoon sugar. Heat mixture over low heat until piping hot, but do not boil. Serve over flat egg noodles.

   Makes four to six servings.

ARTICHOKES FLORENTINE

1 pound fresh spinach
1 teaspoon salt
½ teaspoon white pepper
½ cup heavy cream
1 tablespoon brandy or Cognac
¼ cup butter or margarine
¼ cup flour
1 teaspoon salt
2½ cups milk, scalded
½ cup Gruyere cheese, coarsley grated
¼ cup Parmesan cheese, grated
1 teaspoon dry Sherry
3 cans (8 ounces each) artichoke
  bottoms, drained

1. Rinse, drain, and chop spinach.

2. Place spinach in a heavy saucepan. Add salt, pepper, cream, and brandy. Simmer over low heat, about 20 minutes, stirring often, until spinach is well cooked and mixture has thickened.

3. Melt butter in another saucepan. Stir in flour and salt and cook one minute, stirring constantly.

4. Remove from heat and stir in hot milk. Return to heat and cook, stirring constantly, until mixture comes to a boil and is thickened.

5. Add Gruyere cheese, Parmesan cheese, and Sherry. Blend well.

6. Place drained artichoke bottoms on a broiling pan or flat baking sheet. Pile spinach mixture on top of artichokes. Cover with cheese sauce. Sprinkle with additional cheese, if desired.

7. Run baking dish under a hot broiler just until mixture is piping hot and lightly browned.

Makes four to six servings.

STUFFED VEAL ROLLS (Saltimbocca)

1½ pounds (12 slices) veal shoulder,
    rump, or leg, sliced and pounded
    paper-thin
½ pound (24 slices) prosciutto or ham
½ pound (12 thin slices) mozzarella,
    fontina, provolone, or Swiss cheese
¼ cup butter or margarine
¼ teaspoon sage
¼ teaspoon basil
½ cup Marsala or sherry wine
Parsley, chopped
Parmesan cheese, grated

1. Top each slice of veal with 2 small slices ham and 1 slice of cheese. Roll meat to completely enclose filling, turning in the sides. Secure with string or toothpicks.

2. Heat butter in a large skillet. Add sage and basil. Brown veal rolls on all sides, about five minutes. Remove from skillet and keep warm.

3. Add wine to skillet and boil rapidly for two minutes, scraping brown bits from pan.

4. Return rolls to skillet. Cover and simmer 10 minutes.

5. Remove ties from rolls. Arrange on a heated serving platter. Pour mixture from skillet over top of meat. Sprinkle with parsley and Parmesan cheese.

Makes six servings.

CARROTS A LA CYNGE

2 pounds carrots, peeled and cut up
1 cup heavy cream
6 tablespoons butter
1 teaspoon nutmeg
Dash ginger
Dash salt

1. Cook carrots in a small amount of boiling salted water until tender. Drain.

2. Put carrots and remaining ingredients into a blender or food processor and puree.

3. Reheat mixture in top part of a double boiler over boiling water before serving.

Makes six servings.

PITTSBURGH CHEESE POTATOES

3 baking potatoes
1 package (3 ounces) cream cheese,
    or 1½ cups Cheddar cheese, grated
Butter
Salt
Pepper
Fresh parsley, finely chopped
Bacon bits (optional)

1. Scrub potatoes. Prick with a fork in several places. Bake in a 450 degree oven 45 to 50 minutes or until soft.

2. Remove from oven and when cool enough to handle, cut potatoes in half lengthwise. Scoop out insides, leaving skins intact.

3. Mash potatoes and mix with cream or Cheddar cheese. Add butter, salt, pepper, and parsley to taste. Add bacon bits, if desired.

4. Put mixture back into potato skins. Return to hot 450 degree oven just long enough for tops of potatoes to become lightly browned.

Makes six servings.

SWEET AND SOUR RED CABBAGE

1 medium head red cabbage, cored
    and thinly sliced
2 large apples, peeled and quartered
1 onion, peeled and sliced
1 tablespoon bacon fat
1 teaspoon salt
½ cup sugar
1 cup vinegar
1½ cups water
1 bay leaf
2 whole allspice berries
2 whole cloves

1. Toss together cabbage, apples, and onion.

2. Melt bacon fat in a large skillet. Add salt, sugar, vinegar, water, bay leaf, allspice, and cloves. Add cabbage mixture to skillet and toss lightly. Simmer 90 minutes or until cabbage is very tender and mixture is well cooked. Do not cover skillet during cooking time.

3. Remove bay leaf, allspice, and cloves before serving.

Makes six servings.

CARDINALS ELEGANT CARROTS

¼ cup sugar
1½ teaspoons cornstarch
2 tablespoons lemon juice
2 tablespoons water
1 tablespoon soy sauce
1 pound carrots
3 tablespoons salad oil
½ green pepper
½ cup walnuts, coarsely broken

1. Combine sugar, cornstarch, lemon juice, water, and soy sauce in a small saucepan. Bring to a boil, stirring, and cook one minute until thick and clear. Set aside.

2. Peel carrots and cut into 2-inch finger-sized pieces. Place in a saucepan that has a tight-fitting cover. Add oil and stir lightly. Cover and cook over very low heat about 20 minutes.

3. Remove seeds from green pepper and cut into 2-inch-long strips. Add to carrots, then add sauce, and continue cooking for five minutes. Stir in walnuts. Cook five more minutes.

Makes four servings.

RAIDERS FLAMING SWEET POTATOES

½ cup walnut halves
⅓ cup butter or margarine, melted
1 cup brown sugar, firmly packed
½ teaspoon salt
½ cup orange juice
6 medium sweet potatoes, cooked
⅓ cup brandy

1. Saute walnuts in melted butter, over medium heat, until lightly browned; remove walnuts from skillet.

2. Add brown sugar, salt, and orange juice to butter in skillet. Bring to a boil for three to four minutes.

3. Peel and halve sweet potatoes. Add to syrup with walnuts. Heat gently, basting with syrup during cooking time.

4. Heat brandy over hot water or very low heat. Pour over potatoes and ignite with a kitchen match.

Makes six servings.

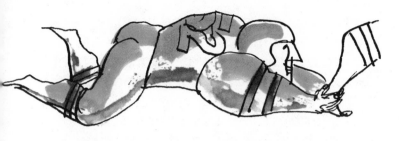

TACKLER'S SQUASH SOUFFLÉ

1½ pounds yellow squash, cleaned and
  cut up
1 large onion, finely chopped
1 egg
½ cup milk
2 tablespoons sugar
½ cup Cheddar cheese, shredded

1. Put squash and onion in a sauce-pan. Add water. Cook about 20 minutes or until tender.

2. Drain thoroughly. Mash squash. Add egg, milk, and sugar and beat until smooth. Stir in grated cheese.

3. Turn mixture into a one-quart casserole.

4. Bake in a 325 degree oven 30 to 40 minutes or until firm.

Makes four to six servings.

FALCONS PECAN PIE

2 eggs
2 tablespoons milk
1 teaspoon vanilla
½ cup brown sugar, firmly packed
¼ cup granulated sugar
1 teaspoon flour
½ cup butter or margarine, melted
1 cup whole pecans
1 9-inch unbaked pie shell

1. Preheat oven to 325 degrees.

2. Beat eggs thoroughly. Add milk, vanilla, brown sugar, white sugar, and flour. Beat well. Mix in butter or margarine. Fold in nuts.

3. Pour mixture into pie shell.

4. Bake 35 to 45 minutes or until fill-ing is firm. Cool before cutting.

BAKED ALASKA

1 quart ice cream, slightly softened
1 pint sherbet
1 8-inch yellow cake layer, homemade
    or purchased
5 egg whites
¾ cup sugar

1. Line a one and a half quart mixing bowl with waxed paper or aluminum foil. Pack slightly softened ice cream along bottom and sides of bowl. Fill center with sherbet. Place a piece of waxed paper on top of ice cream and press flat. Freeze until very firm.

2. Cut out a double layer of heavy brown paper at least one inch larger than the cake layer. Place paper on a baking sheet; place cake layer on paper and chill.

3. Beat egg whites until they form soft peaks. Slowly add sugar, about 2 tablespoonfuls at a time and continue beating until whites are stiff and glossy.

4. Preheat oven to 450 degrees.

5. Invert ice cream onto cake layer and peel off paper. Quickly cover ice cream and cake completely with meringue. At this point the whole Alaska can be returned to freezer and kept until dessert time to bake or it can be baked and served at once.

6. Bake four to five minutes or just until meringue is delicately browned. Place Alaska on a chilled platter and serve immediately.

Makes six to eight servings.

COACH'S CHEESECAKE

18 single graham crackers
⅓ cup butter or margarine, melted
⅛ teaspoon cinnamon
Dash of nutmeg
3 large eggs
¾ cup sugar
3 packages (8 ounces each) cream
    cheese, at room temperature
2 teaspoons vanilla, divided
2 cups dairy sour cream
⅓ cup sugar

1. Oil the bottom of a 9-inch springform pan. Place crackers in a

plastic bag and crush with a rolling pin. Pour into a bowl. Add butter, cinnamon, and nutmeg. Blend thoroughly. Press firmly on bottom of springform pan.

2. Beat eggs with mixer at low speed until well blended. Gradually add ¾ cup sugar and beat until thickened. Cut cream cheese in chunks and add gradually to mixture. Continue beating until mixture is very smooth. Add 1 teaspoon of the vanilla. Pour into springform pan.

3. Bake in a 350 degree oven for 45 minutes or until cake is fairly firm. Remove cake from oven. Turn oven up to 450 degrees.

4. Combine sour cream, ⅓ cup sugar, and remaining teaspoon of vanilla. Spread mixture gently over top of cheesecake. Bake four to five minutes or just until topping is set.

5. Remove from oven and cool on wire rack. Refrigerate overnight before serving.

MEADOWLANDS APPLE MOUSSE

2 pounds tart apples
1 tablespoon unsalted butter
Rind of ½ lemon, grated
¼ cup honey
1 envelope unflavored gelatin
¼ cup cold water
1 teaspoon lemon juice
1 cup heavy cream

1. Peel and core apples. Chop very fine.

2. Melt butter in a heavy saucepan. Add apples and cook slowly to bring out the juice. Turn up heat and cook until apples are cooked to a pulp, stirring occasionally. Add lemon rind and continue cooking until mixture is a thick puree.

3. Remove from heat. Add honey. Soften gelatin in cold water for five minutes. Stir into hot apple mixture until gelatin is dissolved. Add lemon juice. Cool mixture.

4. Whip cream until almost stiff. Fold into apple mixture. Turn mixture into six dessert glasses. Chill.

INDEX